GIVING ADVICE TO STUDENTS:
A Road Map for College Professionals

Howard K. Schein   Ned Scott Laff   Deborah R. Allen

A Publication of the
American College Personnel Association
Media Publication No. 44

ISBN 1-55620-039-0

Publication Sales: Order Services Department
American Association for Counseling and Development
5999 Stevenson Avenue
Alexandria, Virginia 22304

Cover Design by Robb Springfield

Credits
The essays in Chapters 3–6 are adapted from newspaper articles that appeared in *The Daily Illini* (© 1985), copyrighted by the Illini Media Company. The essays in Chapter 7 are modified from self-help brochures produced by the Counseling Center of the University of Illinois at Urbana-Champaign and are copyrighted by the Board of Trustees, University of Illinois. All essays are used with permission of these copyright holders.

TABLE OF CONTENTS

PROLOGUE

This book grew out of a series of articles that we wrote for the *Daily Illini*, the student newspaper at the University of Illinois at Urbana-Champaign. The intent behind the original articles was to introduce basic advising "tricks of the trade" to a large population of undergraduates. Our hope was that by giving students advising basics they would become active members of the campus community and learn how to use their colleges and universities better.

At the same time, we were concerned with a larger issue that we felt was critical to the quality of undergraduate education. Grites (1979) sums it up best:

> It is obvious that the two (student and academic affairs) cannot work in isolation. Just as faculty cannot be mere advancers of a single discipline without affecting their students' personal lives, neither can student affairs professionals develop students independent of their academic lives. (p. 26)
>
> . . . academic affairs and student affairs personnel need to seek each other's cooperation and support. Academic advising can serve as a kind of magnetic thread to mend the historical rift between these two constituencies and to draw the best elements of each to provide students with a better college experience. (p. 30)

Many of the concepts developed in our newspaper series address Grites's concern. Several faculty and student affairs colleagues at the University of Illinois urged us to present these concepts more formally in a practical advising text for a professional audience. This book represents that effort.

The hub of our approach is students' needs. With this focus, the rift between academic affairs and student affairs is diminished and the need for cooperation is magnified. But we have also included a second, crucial "magnetic thread": root concepts and critical thinking skills, which underlie all learning. By incorporating this thread into an advising context we can fit academic advising into a larger, developmentally based scheme of advice giving. With this scheme, we discuss five central elements: academic decision making, resource identification and use, career search, postgraduate studies, and counseling.

ACKNOWLEDGMENTS

Many people contributed their labor, ideas, and support to this book. Roland Holmes and Myles Berman helped us develop many of our ideas during the years we worked with them at the Individual Plans of Study Program at the University of Illinois. They also criticized early drafts. Ralph Trimble coauthored the counseling chapter; Eleanor Markey helped prepare one of the articles in that chapter. Ira Pilchen was our advisee, *Daily Illini* editor, idea generator, and consulting editor on this text. His contributions have been invaluable. Gary North gave us much encouragement to write the book. Glenn Aber and Deborah Green's critiques helped us keep student affairs and student issues highlighted. Robert Copeland and Ralph Page gave us crucial support and encouragement.

Finally, we give our deepest thanks to Pat Talbot who not only prepared this manuscript, but whose kindness of spirit perhaps best characterizes the ambience of empathic advice giving.

ABOUT THE AUTHORS

Deborah R. Allen is associate director and clinical counselor at the Counseling Center of the University of Illinois, Urbana-Champaign. She has been a registered psychologist in the state of Illinois since 1979. She received a BA in psychology from the University of Vermont, and her MA and PhD in clinical psychology from Michigan State University. She has taught paraprofessional training courses, coauthored a series of self-help brochures for students that are marketed nationally, and developed workshops for faculty and teaching assistants on identifying and referring troubled students. She has presented and published nationally and regionally on topics such as self-help programs for students, organizational conflict and change, needs assessment, and a variety of counseling issues.

Ned Scott Laff is currently writing his second book, *Aspects of the Language of Poetry*. He has held positions as assistant dean for freshmen at St. Lawrence University and assistant director of Unit One/Living-Learning Center at the University of Illinois, Urbana-Champaign. Laff received a BA in English from the University of Illinois, Urbana-Champaign, an MA in English and composition from the University of Wyoming, and a PhD in educational policy studies from the University of Illinois, Urbana-Champaign. He has been an adviser in liberal arts and individual plans of study and has presented and published nationally and regionally in the areas of academic advising, literary education, and theory of composition.

Eleanor Markey is a child care worker at the Jewish Children's Bureau in Chicago. She received a BA in psychology from the University of Illinois, Urbana-Champaign, where she worked as a Counseling Center paraprofessional.

Howard K. Schein is director of Unit One/Living-Learning Center, a residence hall-based academic program cosponsored by student affairs and academic affairs at the University of Illinois, Urbana-Champaign. He is also assistant director of housing for academic programs. He received a BA in biology from Grinnell College, an MA in zoology from the University of California, Berkeley, and a PhD in zoology from the University of Illinois, Urbana-Champaign. He has been a liberal arts adviser and has presented and published nationally and regionally in the areas of student development, academic advising, and marine invertebrate behavior. He is currently on the editorial board of the National Academic Advising Association (NACADA) Journal.

Ralph W. Trimble is director and clinical counselor at the Counseling Center of the University of Illinois, Urbana-Champaign. He has been a registered psychologist in the state of Illinois since 1974. He received a BS in psychology from the University of Iowa and a PhD in clinical psychology from the University of Illinois, Urbana-Champaign. He has taught paraprofessional training courses, and has presented and published nationally and regionally on topics such as test anxiety and suicide prevention. He has served as an organizational management consultant and is on the steering committee of the Association of University and College Counseling Center Directors.

INTRODUCTION

Every road traveler has a personal style. Some speed toward their destinations; others travel more slowly, enjoying the scenery along the way. Some prefer to drive superhighways; others prefer backcountry roads. The superhighways are fast, efficient routes to enable travelers to get from here to there. They are relatively safe routes to travel—help is easy to find, roads are marked clearly, and the choices are few. Even detours are easy to follow. They put you back in the fast lane with little fuss or bother. A standard road map is all that is usually needed.

Back-roads travel is quite different. Travelers cannot simply set their cars on cruise control and speed down the highway. They have to pay attention to road signs, traffic, and hidden turns. Detours spring out of nowhere, and seat-of-the-pants navigation skills are frequently required. Standard road maps may become useless as road signs become few and far between. Sometimes back-roads travelers become utterly lost and confused to the point that explicit directions from locals are necessary to find the way. But locals can help back-roads travelers experience a lot more than finding the right roads. The general store operator can tell you how to get to the hidden hot springs to soak your body, and the antique dealer can lead you to the best home cooking in the county. The only road maps that come to the rescue are the ones made during the trip.

TRAVELING THROUGH COLLEGE

These styles of travel parallel how students "travel" through colleges and universities. Most students tend to look at their college program catalogs as the "guide maps" to the "superhighways" that will take them through school. But good education does not always lend itself to obvious road maps and superhighway travel. To get a good education it is necessary to have the ability to travel many different kinds of roads, read and make maps, and know when and where to stop for advice.

One problem is that campus professionals who give advice do not necessarily have the same styles of travel, the same road maps, or comparable map reading skills. For example, faculty and student affairs professionals do not share a singular view of what college life is about. Faculty roles lie in academic realms—teaching and research. Student affairs roles lie in developmental realms—talking with students about their personal concerns. Although their maps may overlap at times, they often differ significantly.

Over the course of their years in college students will develop map reading skills, personal maps, and map making skills. Usually, however, students begin college by relying on maps given to them by faculty and student affairs professionals. But faculty and student affairs professionals sometimes give students different kinds of maps and leave students on their own to interpret how these maps overlap. Thus, students may have difficulty developing clear and personally meaningful maps for their educations.

THE AIM OF THIS BOOK

This book is designed to help faculty and student affairs professionals blend their expertise in order to help students integrate their college experiences. The goal is to help students become capable of setting their own directions and mapping their own routes, while knowing how and where to get help at all stages of their development and at all levels of difficulty in their travels.

PREMISES AND OBJECTIVES

Two premises underlie this book. The first is that students often do not make optimal use of their colleges and universities because they are not acquainted with the underlying principles of academic life. The second is that the tasks of working through the academic structure, planning a satisfying undergraduate education, and learning how to use academic resources are developmental processes that can make college a rewarding individual growth experience.

Based upon these premises, this book has two major objectives. The first is to use students' needs as the focal point for demonstrating how academic and student affairs issues are wedded. The second is to present a scheme for teaching students self-advising skills and strategies.

ONE OVERRIDING THEME

Much of what campus professionals take for granted is not obvious to students. Campus professionals frequently fail to incorporate their "givens" into the thoughts they share, the questions they ask, and the programs they plan for and with students. Academic settings offer many different types of activities, tend to be supportive of high-risk ventures, and are generally accepting of idiosyncratic ways of expression and problem solving. Knowing this, it is easy to assume that students will use their years at college to try new things, test ideas, venture into new areas, and possibly fail at times. After all, in few other evaluative settings are nonsuccesses padded so softly. But these and other assumptions are not always obvious to students. By sharing our assumptions with students, they may be challenged and encouraged to take advantage of the unusual freedom to explore that is inherent in academic settings.

HOW THIS BOOK IS ORGANIZED

This book is written for campus professionals who would like some critical advising hints. Chapters may be read in the order presented or according to the reader's interest.

Chapter 1 discusses an intersection for academic and student affairs. Chapter 2 describes the common ground underlying these two sectors. The intent behind these two chapters is to sketch out an advising philosophy that blends academic and student affairs concerns and provides a practical advising framework.

Chapters 3–7 each consist of two parts. The first part presents conceptual and practical approaches to each problem area. The second part consists of short essays that are meant to stimulate and, at times, provoke the reader. Sometimes the essays are philosophical, sometimes they are opinions, and sometimes they are instructive. At all times they urge readers to think about and question the personal relevance of their views of college. These essays contain information that campus professionals need to know and need to be able to communicate to students. They are written in a style that makes them readily usable as articles in campus newspapers, as individual handouts, or as residence hall posters. Each of these chapters challenges a commonly held belief that confronts students and campus professionals:

- In chapter 3 the belief that academic majors should be developed primarily in response to the structure of academic departments is countered with the concept of "fields of study."

- In chapter 4 the belief that campus resources are easily accessible to students is challenged by demonstrating the "invisibility" of many resources and by suggesting strategies for making resources visible.
- In chapter 5 the belief that vocational issues are solely in the hands of career specialists is addressed by suggesting strategies for incorporating creative academic choices, internship study, and noncredit activities into the career exploration process.
- In chapter 6 the belief that applying to graduate or professional school is a process of reading catalogs and mailing transcripts is challenged with a comprehensive search strategy that involves diverse information sources.
- In chapter 7 the belief that only counselors can help with counseling problems is addressed by providing a "how-to" manual that introduces basic counseling and referral skills.

This book is written from a peer perspective. The authors are active advisers and counselors who have both academic backgrounds and student affairs experience. Their views of what advising can be and the contributions it can make are culled from years of practical experience. This book is intended to be a translation of practical skills and common sense into the advising arena. No attempt has been made to include an exhaustive literature review. Grites (1979) has done a thorough job in this area and provides a good foundation for all campus professionals. Explicit references to conceptual approaches to developmental issues are also absent from this text. These issues are thoroughly addressed by Winston, Miller, Ender, Grites, & Associates (1984). Their text provides a basic foundation in student development theory as it applies to academic advising.

The text distinguishes between "advisers," who are commonly thought of as "academic advisers," and a more encompassing group, "advice givers." All members of the academic community—faculty, student affairs professionals, administrators, paraprofessionals, students, and the like—are potential advice givers to students. The text, then, is not directed to a single audience but to the common interests among advice givers. Depending on readers' areas of expertise, they may find certain chapters to be new and others to be more basic. Either way, readers have several options for using these chapters. Faculty readers, for instance, may find chapter 3, "The Myth of the Academic Major," basic to their understanding of academic disciplines. Faculty can use this chapter to give students and student affairs professionals insight into the rationale behind departmental majors. Likewise, readers with counseling backgrounds may find the concepts presented in chapter 7, "A Primer on Counseling Skills," to be rather obvious. However, the chapter can serve as a useful handbook for training paraprofessionals or for teaching basic skills to faculty.

For paraprofessional readers, this text provides a foundation for the issues confronting their peers and themselves. It can be used as a basic text in their training. It can also be used in counseling and college student personnel programs as a stimulus for discussion of important campus issues.

This text is meant to be an all-purpose handbook. It is intended to be instructive and contentious. It is designed to stimulate dialogue and to stimulate a process of questioning the traditional assumptions and roles of advice givers on college campuses. This process will enhance advice givers' capabilities, which is the central purpose of this book.

CHAPTER 1

ADVICE GIVING AND THE QUALITY OF EDUCATION

Most students do not actively design their academic experiences. Instead, they tend to be passive recipients of what they are taught. They depend, in large part, on note taking as their primary classroom learning technique and on college course and program descriptions as their primary guides to their college careers. Thus, many students graduate with neither the content nor the process of a broad-based education and without the skills they need for independent, self-guided learning. The undergraduate education most students experience, then, is a cluster of isolated experiences lacking sound cohesiveness.

THE SHORTSIGHTEDNESS OF ACADEMIC AFFAIRS

The hub of activity on any campus is academic affairs. Most institutional mission statements reflect this focus, and it filters from the president's office down through the faculty and staff. But ironically, this academic mission seems to lose its impact when students, especially lower-division undergraduates, are considered. In part, this failure is due to a common short sight on the part of many in academic affairs about the nature of students' undergraduate lives.

For many students, undergraduate education means more than academic coursework. It means the full range of educational opportunities and experiences they encounter during their undergraduate years. Academic and intellectual growth are only parts of a larger personal development experience. What institutions may fail to consider in thinking about their educational missions is that students' personal development has a direct impact on their readiness to pursue academic and intellectual goals.

1

STUDENT AFFAIRS IN THE ACADEMIC COMMUNITY

Student affairs traditionally has been considered supportive to rather than collegial with academic affairs. Perhaps, because of this, student affairs often has found itself left out of the process of operationally defining institutions' educational goals. As a result, student affairs professionals may not be well versed in academic issues and may lack credibility with those in academic affairs.

Yet student affairs professionals tend to interact with students more often and more personally than do most faculty and departmental advisers. Student affairs professionals may, therefore, be in a unique position to facilitate students' access to their colleges and universities. Despite this position, when they attempt to give educational advice, student affairs professionals often find themselves at loggerheads with those in the academic realm.

TWO SEPARATE GROUPS

A perceived division of labor and expertise between those people concerned with research and scholarly concerns (academic affairs) and those concerned with student development and personal problem solving (student affairs) often creates two distinct campus groups. The contrast between the two is instructive.

When faculty serve as academic advice givers, their strength usually lies in describing and discussing the academic nature of their departments. Their expertise usually lies within their respective areas of research. Although faculty advisers may be adept with problems of course selection and departmental requirements, they may never have been taught to help students integrate their coursework with career and life plans. Faculty advisers' weakness in this area is notable (Katchadourian & Boli, 1985). But faculty are not likely to take the time to become proficient in these areas unless the academic system changes dramatically to give them the time, training, and appropriate rewards.

Student affairs professionals' advice on educational planning often tends to be procedurally oriented—aimed at helping students negotiate the rules, and developmentally oriented—aimed at helping students make personal sense of their decisions. But these professionals rarely have the faculty's expertise in specific areas of academic inquiry or the ability to share insights about the subtleties of academic scholarship.

The result of these differences is that those who occupy the realms of academic and student affairs often feel they do not have the expertise to work in each other's areas. Students, therefore, face a collegiate structure that compartmentalizes their experiences. They are often presented with a "dis-integrated" environment and are left on their own to integrate it. This can result in students' feeling that their college experiences are disruptively fragmented.

CREATING A BRIDGE: DEVELOPMENTAL ADVISING

Advice givers can avoid contributing to this fragmentation in students' lives by being holistic. They can take responsibility for helping students integrate their college experiences by blending the expertise of both academic affairs and student affairs. This blending is the underlying theme of developmental advising, an approach that incorporates basic student development theory into academic advising strategies.

In its broadest sense, developmental advising focuses "on identifying and accomplishing life goals, acquiring skills and attitudes that promote intellectual and personal growth, and sharing concerns for each other and the academic community" (Ender, Winston, & Miller, 1984, p. 19). Developmental advising teaches advice givers to look at students as complete individuals at different levels of personal growth, and argues that a critical role of academic advice giving is to foster personal as well as educational growth.

An assumption of developmental advising is that academic and student affairs have overlapping concerns. In embracing developmental advising concepts, academic affairs and student affairs become colleagues in cooperative efforts that positively affect students. Using developmental advising as the bridge between academic affairs and student affairs requires two steps. First, advice givers need to understand and pay attention to both the "academic way of being" and students' developmental processes in order to help students make optimal use of their academic settings. Second, advice givers need to know basic strategies and common sense approaches so that they can work with students within a broad range of issues without feeling they have to defer to "experts." In cases where students' needs truly go beyond advice givers' abilities, however, advice givers must recognize this and refer students to appropriate experts, just as general medical practitioners must direct their clients and patients to medical specialists.

The task, then, is to help student affairs professionals and faculty build a bridge that incorporates the concerns of both academic affairs and student affairs but with students' needs as the focal point.

This bridge is grounded on three major components: first, on a set of basic skills and concepts that provides a framework for both academic inquiry and general problem solving (chapter 2); second, on the challenge

3

to one of the fundamental assumptions that governs how advice givers and students think about educational planning—the "myth of the academic major" (chapter 3); and third, on the assumption that all campus advice givers can develop a set of skills that enables them to be viable advice-giving general practitioners (chapters 4–7).

CHAPTER 2

FINDING A COMMON GROUND

"Root concepts" (Lauer & Hussey, 1986) and "critical thinking skills" (Arons, 1985) are frameworks that underlie all learning—from faculty research agendas to students' life-planning concerns. Although frameworks like these are most commonly utilized in the academic arena, they are equally important in advice giving. Yet advice givers rarely take the time to work with students in ways that utilize these concepts. This chapter will illustrate the features that make up these concepts within the context of advice giving.

ROOT CONCEPTS

Root concepts are the frameworks on which people "hang" the information they generate and are the frameworks for building interconnections. The basic components are three interrelated concepts: relation, order, and structure.

Relation

Seeing how parts interact, how they relate, enables people to make inferences to other situations. Take, for example, the current societal concern about drug abuse. Should drug use be analyzed from a unidimensional viewpoint or should the relationship of drug abuse to its political, social, cultural, and economic factors be considered? Can history provide clues to recurring patterns that relate the use of drugs in various cultures and societies to the problems of today? And, knowing how these relationships are drawn, can parallel relationships be seen when the word "poverty" is substituted for "drugs?"

Can advice givers help students see relationships between their current personal situations and personal situations that will confront them in the future? How do the skills gained from confronting and solving roommate and floor mate conflicts, as opposed to changing roommates or ignoring these conflicts, relate to solving marital and family problems, rather than resorting to divorce? And how do these interpersonal problem-solving issues relate to more generalized situations, such as community and global conflict?

Can students be helped to see the relationships between curricular goals and how the world actually behaves? Is medicine solely a study of biology and chemistry, or should clinical, scientific, social, cultural, psychological, and economic issues be considered as well?

Relation has to do with common denominators. For advice giving, the focus should be on cohesion, integration, composition, and the like. How do departmental major requirements and general education requirements relate to each other in a way that makes sense in a student's educational plans? What are the correlations among general education requirements? How do they provide a broad-based education but at the same time provide a coherent perspective? These are not difficult questions.

Advice givers need to keep in mind that course patterns can represent multiple relations. For example, coursework in cultural anthropology, introductory ethics, social psychology, and economics added to coursework in biology, chemistry, and mathematics can provide a broad-based course structure for pursuing the study of social perspectives in medical care/premed. Similarly, those same courses can provide a basis for studying science, technology, and human values. Another example revolves around the incorporation of mathematics into a student's curriculum. Many degree programs in the sciences and social sciences have minimal mathematics requirements. How students decide whether to continue with mathematics should be related to the level of expertise they seek. Differentiation and statistics are mathematical tools that provide potential for sophisticated levels of analysis in many fields. Students, however, frequently do not see this until they are shown how these components relate.

In a different context, advice givers can help students analyze the anxiety they feel when taking tests in courses that their parents pressured them to choose. Is this anxiety related to performance pressure or parental pressure? In what other areas do these students feel anxiety when performance or parental approval are issues?

Order

How parts relate is only one critical aspect of this scheme. Students also have to learn to deal with consequences. For advice givers this means, in large part, helping students develop some sort of "foresight." By learning the importance of the concept of order students can extrapolate from present situations to future possibilities. Advice givers cannot let students believe that a broad-based education is applicable to many career paths simply because they learn to read, write, and think, or that a resume loaded with long lists of unconnected and empty activities will contribute to personal skill building and impressive credentials. Relationships are built from components that are sequentially or causally connected. Is it important that one thing come before another? For instance, when developing credentials for a resume, should students consider joining several organizations during their freshman year, drop some and commit to others during their sophomore year, and move into leadership positions of a select one or two later on?

What consequences can the order of courses have, for instance, for an English major? The consequences can be significant, and they may be illustrated by talking with students about a simple point—"What does being an English major mean?" Students can study fiction, drama, or poetry. They can approach these from analytical frameworks of archetypal criticism, psychology, Marxism, feminism, existentialism, poststructuralism, and so on. Students can prepare for graduate study, communications, public relations, or other professional study. Each of these involves reading, writing, and thinking, and each provides a broad-based education. But each focus involves a different ordering of courses, different courses to fill general education and elective hours, and different consequences for the student's overall undergraduate program.

Structure

This leads to the final component—structure. Structure is the tool for seeing how parts are put together and where parts are needed. By learning how to discern or create structure, students can put the concepts of relation and order into a common framework. What are the known components of a scheme? Where are new components needed (relation) and when or how do they fit in (order)?

By knowing about structure, students can also gain insight into processes and outcomes. What are the implications of student governments built on elected representatives and executive boards versus governments built on "town meetings" and committees with members having vested interests in the committees' actions? Helping students to uncover their colleges' governing structures helps them to find their places on campus committees. It may also help students learn to generalize their understandings of governing structures to their own concerns about student government, and, potentially, to their concerns about all forms of government.

Structure plays a critical role in the academic advising process. Consider international relations. At many colleges this is an area of study that melds courses in the humanities, the arts, history, political science, economics, geography, and foreign language. Properly balanced, a program of this kind should be sensitive to and critical of the complexities of relationships among cultures, nations, and nation-states. Although the need to blend in a field like international relations is fairly obvious, it is no different than how we should be helping students learn to plan their studies in English, chemistry, or business administration.

CRITICAL THINKING

Critical thinking is a process by which information is generated. A 10-part scheme developed by Arons (1985) is condensed, here, into 5 components that fit advice-giving contexts. The components are (a) consciously raising questions; (b) becoming aware of gaps in information; (c) probing assumptions; (d) drawing inferences; and (e) testing conclusions.

Consciously Raising Questions

When integrating critical thinking skills into an advice-giving framework, the first step is to consciously raise questions with students. The intent is to make students feel a bit uneasy. Without this uneasiness students may make decisions complacently. Even students who are undecided majors may fall prey to complacency. Advice givers need to help them ask themselves what they know about "academic majors"; how they know what makes up a program of study; what their attitudes are about people from dissimilar backgrounds; what the motivating factors are that drive them; what they take for granted, and, perhaps most importantly, what they bring with them that governs the way they think about their college educations. By raising questions like these advice givers often discover that the majority of students, including juniors and seniors, do not know how to think about what they want to do in their college settings.

Consider students who want to major in business because they believe that without a business degree they will not be able to land a job when they graduate. It is often hard enough to get these students to ask any questions. They may need to be cajoled because they come to school with seemingly firm ideas about their educational paths. Advice givers can, however, help them to question their assumptions by challenging what they think they know. What does it mean to major in business? For that matter, what is business; or, perhaps more appropriately, what isn't business? What does a "business person" do? What personal strengths and interests are related to a career in business?

No single answers to these questions exist because they can be answered in many different ways. Students tailor their approaches to the study of business by how they answer these questions. But many students make their way through school never asking these, or similar questions, or ever having such questions posed to them. They rely on the outlines of education prescribed by their college catalogs and on unfounded views of what awaits them in the world of work. They may never stop to think about the educational sense behind these outlines and views.

Advice givers need to challenge students to rethink their old assumptions so that they do not automatically apply these assumptions in new situations. For instance, residence hall staff frequently bring up the issue of leadership development. By being questioned about what makes a leader, the nature of residence hall communities, and the features of good government, students learn to see alternative models of leadership. This may challenge students to reconsider the forms of student government they experienced in high school. At the same time, staff may help students to see, in the working setting of residence hall life, opportunities to test the models of leadership, government, and participatory management they study in the classroom. By raising questions with answers that beg for student action, advice givers provide students with an arena for turning theory into practice.

Becoming Aware of Gaps in Information

By consciously raising questions with students, advice givers help students become aware of gaps in their information. Gaps in information become apparent whenever students are faced with decisions. Did they have the whole picture from their high school counselors when choosing their particular colleges? Is dropping out of school the only choice when academic times get tough? Is changing roommates the only alternative when problems occur? Are there curricular gaps between the way majors are currently outlined and the projected direction of growth in various fields?

Many colleges and universities lag in keeping their curricula up to date with changes in knowledge, technology, the work place, and the like. Students need to know what parts of their college curricula will prepare them for future career challenges or further study and where those programs may fall short. This is as true for those pursuing careers after their undergraduate years as it is for those planning graduate and professional study.

Rarely do advice givers question how changes in fields of study or curricular policy may affect undergraduates' careers or educational goals. Is the best way to prepare for medical school through a life sciences major or are other fields more professionally and personally relevant? Do MBA programs prefer business majors, or is any undergraduate major admissible? Is a resume stacked with "extras" attractive to prospective employers, or are these employers looking for evidence of substance?

Advice givers need to teach students to build frames of reference that help them recognize the difference between belief based on hearsay, opinion, or just plain guesswork and knowledge that supports their beliefs. In the academic realm students need to know that faculty, not curricula, keep pace with changes. Advice givers need to encourage students to fill gaps with independent study or internships.

Probing Assumptions

Students need to learn to probe their assumptions so they never take anything for granted. Unwarranted assumptions may provide a false foundation for any endeavor. Yet such assumptions are often abundant in undergraduate mythologies: that political science or business is the "appropriate" pre-law curriculum; that only mentally ill people seek help from psychological counselors; that a major leading to a high-paying job will also lead to personal satisfaction and happiness.

Student development theory (e.g., Perry, 1970) points to a helpful dimension of this issue. Frequently, young undergraduates' assumptions are framed by their beliefs that a "correct way" exists, that the world is framed in right/wrong concepts and yes/no answers. Such assumptions can be difficult to probe. The act of probing, however, can entice them to see the relative nature of things and that a particular assumption might be one of many. The probing may pay off by opening new pathways to potential courses of action (i.e., by providing choices).

Drawing Inferences

Students need to learn how to draw inferences from the information they gather. By teaching students to ask questions, to look at gaps in their information, and to probe assumptions, advice givers teach students how to "critically read" their worlds and make informed observations. Advice givers next need to help students put those observations into a context of "If . . . then." What inferences can students draw from new trends in research, technology, and the marketplace? How do these trends affect the interrelatedness of academic disciplines? How does the burgeoning emphasis on personal fitness affect the integration of sports, kinesiology, medicine, sociology, economics, and business administration? What are the current uses of computer technology? How does "international relations" parcel out into areas of language, culture, geography, economics, and political science? And, on a more individual level, how do personal interests, strengths, and dreams translate into a plan that fits into curricular parameters?

The answers to these questions are not as difficult as they may first seem. Sometimes the answers come directly from an insightful reading of the newspaper where obvious intersections of fields of interest are illustrated every day. Sports, public relations, and marketing; the fine arts and business; public relations and medicine; and business, social welfare, and interpersonal relations are just a few examples. The point is that advice givers need explicitly to raise the types of questions that help students draw inferences.

Testing Conclusions

Finally, with these four skills in hand, advice givers should challenge students to test their own conclusions. Students need to learn to test their thinking for consistency and coherence. Independent study, research arrangements, internships, informational interviews, and participation in the academic community's noncurricular activities are all avenues where advice givers can direct students to test their thinking. In this way students can begin to take responsibility for their own intellectual growth and can learn to deal with a changing educational scene. The more opportunities students have to test their conclusions, the more informed their decision making will be.

Internships, for example, are usually good places to accomplish some of these goals. Principles learned in class can be readily put to the test in the work place, and students' personal decisions about potential job settings also can be tested. Are theories of management learned in class put to use in the office? "Do I really fit in here like I thought I would?" These tests come easily through internships.

Although root concepts and critical thinking skills are common sense to many of those who work in college settings, these concepts often are not incorporated into advice-giving strategies. Incorporating these concepts requires that advice givers have and take time to explore issues with students, rather than merely passing along information or providing answers. The impact of incorporating these concepts into advice giving is twofold. First, advice givers will have a concrete method for helping students solve problems. Second, advice givers will, by example, teach students a process for solving their own problems.

CHAPTER 3

THE MYTH OF THE ACADEMIC MAJOR

When Eric Shipton climbed Mount Everest in 1953 he chronicled an experience similar to other climbers who had attempted to scale the mountain. The foreign climbers, at home with compasses and map projections, easily matched their views of the peaks and saddles familiar to them from the north face with a view of the mountain from the south. But native Sherpas learned from their culture to see each face of the mountain as a different mountain. Although they had known the features of the north and south faces of Everest from having spent their lives in the shadow of the mountain, the Sherpas had never connected these faces as part of the same mountain. For the Sherpas, the two faces of the mountain were not both Everest. Each face presented a separate picture and puzzle to be solved. They had no way of fitting the two faces together (Bronowski, 1965).

Shipton's account of the Sherpas is an appropriate image for how many approaches to advice giving affect students. Unlike Shipton, however, who helped the Sherpas fit the pieces together to build a map of the mountain, basic strategies in advice giving often leave students with fragmented pictures of their educational plans. This fragmentation is fostered by the most pervasive question with which students are confronted, "What is your major?"

When students are advised to decide upon and work within the prescribed boundaries of "academic majors," discussions are often limited to questions generated by college catalogs. And because students' understanding is prescribed by the way college catalogs describe academic majors, students rarely ask questions about the academic substance of the curricula that constitute those majors. Instead, students tend to focus on semester schedules, fulfilling requirements, and course selection. Issues

13

concerning the content of undergraduate study are usually not on students' agendas. With this prescriptive structure students come to believe that a college's departmental divisions and the basic credit-hour requirements for the majors within these divisions bear some relevance to academic, career, and life-planning choices. Too often this is not the case.

This focus on academic majors all too often undermines students' chances of making sense of their educations. Academic majors, as defined by most college catalogs, offer little insight into the areas of study in which faculty are engaged. Catalogs usually do not provide insight into the fruitful relationships that can exist between personal academic interests and the formalities of college studies. As a result, students usually find it difficult to think about the relationships between their educational interests and what their colleges have to offer.

This is the "myth of the academic major." By encouraging students to plan their educations around academic majors, advice givers may implicitly discourage critical thinking skills and understanding of root concepts. Thus they inadvertently limit students' views of what makes up a college education and, consequently, encourage them to think prescriptively. Students become like the Sherpas, unable to build maps in which the different faces of their educations fit snugly together. To enable students to become map makers of their own educations, advice givers must help them do away with the blinders that the myth of the academic major imposes. Instead students must be introduced to "fields of study."

FIELDS OF STUDY

A field of study is thematically based. Rather than being an outline of basic course competency requirements and required hours, fields of study center on problematic issues or areas of interest and ways to go about studying them. The idea is to coordinate general education courses, required departmental hours, electives, independent study, and internships into a central theme that provides an interdisciplinary understanding of a particular subject area.

The difference between a major and a field of study can be illustrated by drawing a parallel between the administrative entity called department and the individuals who make up the faculty of a department. Just as there are no generic majors there are also no generic professors of, for instance, political science, English, or biology. These professors might, however, work on problems of political economy and resource management, literary stylistics, or immunology. Their academic work reflects interdisciplinary study because of the ways various areas of knowledge provide perspectives on their fields. Just as the salient features of faculty's academic interests delineate fields of study, not academic majors, so advising should help students delineate their fields of study instead of merely negotiating the requirements of academic majors.

HOW TO CONSTRUCT A FIELD OF STUDY

One way to implement the fields-of-study concept is to break the process of defining a field into three parts. Advisers must help students:

1. *Identify what they want to accomplish.*
   - What do they want to know about?
   - How do they go about it?
   - What skills do they want to develop?
   - What are the components of the content and skill areas they have identified?
   - How do the pieces fit together?

2. *Translate the answers to these questions into educational experiences.*
   - What courses, independent study and research agreements, internships, and extracurricular activities will work together to fulfill their content and skill development areas?

3. *Find the academic department that will accommodate these actions.*
   - How do field-of-study course combinations fit into existing departments?
   - Which courses can fill general education and elective requirements?
   - How can independent study agreements fit?
   - What extracurricular activities fill in the gaps that courses do not cover?
   - How can exceptions to rules be arranged in order to accommodate legitimate educational planning?

This approach helps students find more leeway in negotiating through existing departmental structures in order to make their academic plans more personally relevant.

THE FLEXIBILITY OF FIELDS OF STUDY

The flexibility of the field-of-study approach is its strength. Although a field of study may be designed within a single department, it is likely that the same field may be pursued through several departments. The difference lies in the area of emphasis. Consider health policy studies.

This area might be approached through several fields of study such as social perspectives on health care, the economics of health care, or governmental health policy development. Students could include in these fields of study courses in administration, economics, literature and philosophy, political science, sociology, social work, mathematical modeling, and operations research.

Whereas many schools do not have defined majors in health policy studies, most schools have both the components to make up such a program and the flexibility within their departmental requirements to permit students to pursue such a course of study. But this field of study, like many, is hidden and invisible to students when they focus on fulfilling the requirements of academic majors.

Although students still end up fulfilling the requirements of academic majors when they utilize the field-of-study framework, their programs take on a different character. Suddenly, a student is not simply a "sociology major," but someone who is pursuing a field of study in the problems of health care delivery or the social causes of health and illness. Sociology provides the content/skill core and the predominant perspective. But general education, cognate, and elective courses can be coordinated to make that sociology perspective a broader one. For instance, economics courses could provide insight into the costs of health care; philosophy courses could provide insight into ethics, social policy, and moral problems in medicine; anthropology courses could provide insight into how different cultural groups perceive and accept health care. When students realize how different courses contribute to the overall plan of their fields of study, they can build themes into their educations.

Despite the objections of some that this approach teaches students to become too specialized, this approach usually fosters many of the basic aims of a broad-based undergraduate education. With a field-of-study approach students are encouraged to use their general education courses and electives wisely instead of amassing a potpourri of courses that merely fulfill requirements. At the very least, students are taught how to create for themselves interdisciplinary, yet coherent, educations. Students become "specifically general." Their educations are content specific because they focus on fields of study. But at the same time these educations are general in three ways. First, students master critical thinking skills by working on the problems a field-of-study education raises. Second, students gain the skill of learning how to go about learning. These two generalize to all learning endeavors. And third, students do fulfill the curricular requirements mandated by their faculty. The difference is that students create their own rationales for these requirements.

By engaging in this process, students shift their focus away from fulfilling the requirements of majors as outlined by their colleges. Instead, they learn to use college resources in ways that personalize their academic programs. This process gives students a strong stake in their educational outcomes by giving them a sense of empowerment that may result in higher levels of achievement and satisfaction. Finally, because faculty construct departmental majors from the field-of-study rationale, they implicitly employ root concepts (relation, order, and structure) when delineating the courses that make up a major. Advice givers need to be explicit with students about this rationale so that students can both understand what makes up the core studies of academic fields and how studies in other fields as well as other educational experiences fit around these core studies.

BETTER USE OF THE FACULTY

The field-of-study approach to academic planning offers students something else. As discussed earlier, although faculty are not generic professors, students tend to see them as such. In advising sessions students tend to talk with faculty in terms of academic majors and generic faculty roles. By teaching students to think in terms of fields of study, advice givers can begin to help students see faculty for who they are and in the various roles they play. Faculty response is usually positive when a student asks a content question such as "I think I'm interested in interpersonal communications and conflict resolution. Can you help me?" instead of a broadly generic question, "I think I want to major in speech communications. What do I need to take?" With content as a base, faculty can discuss with students how to pursue fields of study. For this to occur, students must be able to "see" their faculty. In too many instances, however, faculty remain "invisible."

An example illustrates these points:

A student questioned what she could "do" with a biology degree if she either did not gain admission to medical school or decided not to try. It never occurred to this student to ask, "Why do I want to be a biology major?" When asked, she realized that she did not want to be a biology major. She wanted to work in a health-oriented field without necessarily being a physical therapist, nurse, or doctor. Here was an undeclared student in a declared major. She never thought to look into the developing trends in health care and how her education might serve the dual purpose of providing her with an intriguing field of study and preparing her for those trends. Moreover, she did not consider that her personal interests could provide her the key to a viable educational plan and that her interests might be shared by faculty who would be willing to work with her. By helping her realize some of the possible relationships among her personal interests in dance and exercise and her educational interests in health she was able to learn to see a field of study—how human performance/exercise physiology could fit into a variety of health-oriented fields.

Equally important, this student was able to identify two faculty members whose interests paralleled hers. The first was her introductory biology professor, who, ironically, was one of the faculty advisers designated by the biology department. This faculty member was also director of the Human Performance Laboratory. His field of study concentrated on the effects of exercise on human physiology. Part of his research looked at the relationships between exercise and health. The student, however, saw this faculty member only as a generic biology professor. As a result, her previous advising contacts with him were oriented toward signing course registration cards. When she began to think of her education in terms of a field of study, she was able to make connections between these "two-people-in-one." This faculty member, instead of being in the dark as to his advisee's interest, was able to help her outline a field of study that included independent study with him.

This student's adviser also referred her to one of his colleagues. This colleague was also interested in the physiological aspects of human physical activity and the effects of exercise on energy capacities, performance, and aging. Yet this faculty member was in the physical education department, a department a biology major would not normally consider investigating. With her adviser's help, this student was able to create a research project with the physical education professor on the relationship between certain types of exercise and the prevention of injuries in dance. The mentoring that started with a field-of-study approach helped this student begin to access the network of the college's hidden resources.

THE PAYOFFS

What does this add up to? Most students, even if they call themselves "declared majors," are undeclared in terms of fields of study. They fulfill requirements for majors but they do not understand what their majors mean. They have missed the opportunity to develop individualized undergraduate programs that are personally and academically satisfying. They have also missed the chance to create academic relationships where faculty serve as field-of-study mentors. Although students are surrounded by a wealth of resources, they are traditionally left on their own to make the appropriate connections.

As advice givers teach students to talk with faculty, advice givers also need to give students the critical thinking skills to raise questions that will allow them to access hidden fields of study. Thinking in terms of academic majors may inhibit that. It is not enough that advice givers, who know how campuses are structured, understand that a major has more administrative than educational relevance. Students believe otherwise. They matriculate with the conviction that academic majors outlined in college catalogs will provide them with all they need to know to plan their educations, explore their career choices, and orient themselves to lifelong learning.

By eliminating the concept of the academic major as the focus of educational planning and replacing it with the idea of fields of study, advice givers can help students look at colleges and universities as learning resources that can be used to achieve their personalized educational, professional, and life goals.

ESSAYS ON ADVISING AND THE NATURE Of COLLEGE STUDIES

The essays in this section address several issues. The first two essays are "pep talks." They present ways to encourage students to make use of their campus resources, to locate advising experts, and to take responsibility for making their own decisions. The third essay outlines a philosophical base for designing a college degree program. The thoughts of this essay are critical to student affairs advice givers who need to understand their academic colleagues, to students who need to know the rationale behind curricula, and to anyone who needs to understand or explain the foundations of college studies. The fourth essay is informative, outlining how to access faculty resources. The final essay is, once again, philosophical, arguing that a broad-based education is essential to the careerist as well as to the intellectual.

Advice givers who wish to incorporate the thoughts of these essays into their interactions with students can readily paraphrase them and may also reproduce these essays for distribution.

Academic advising . . . You've been there. It may have been during the first time you registered for courses, when so much was thrown at you that aspirin and a beer would have made better sense. It may have been while you were trying to add a course, and you spent two days being sent from one office to the next— getting the grand tour of the campus—simply to drop off your course registration form at your college office.

It may have been during that time of year when timetables come out and you sat searching for that spectacular array of courses that would satisfy general education requirements, department requirements, and let you sleep until 10 a.m. It may have been when you were sitting at the registrar's desk being told about the courses that would not quite fit the requirements, or when the dean told you that your sad story was like all the rest, and that you'd be around an extra semester. It may have been when you decided that your college advising system isn't what it's cracked up to be.

And your adviser, if you know who he or she is, always seems amenable to signing your course request and giving you a minute or two during the enrollment flood. When asked, you can always say that you have seen your adviser at least once a semester. Academic advising . . . obtaining it always seems like a three-ring circus during course registration time.

But now we come along and lay this worn-out cliché on you: Good academic advising can be the cornerstone of a solid and personally rewarding college career. In some instances, it can save your academic life. And—get this one—it can help you search out and put to use the resources and educational possibilities a college or university has to offer.

That's all well and good, but who is going to work this little miracle? Why, you are! You see, like everything else on a campus, advisers are resources, not ultimate authorities. They don't have to live with the program of study you devise—you do. And that means you have the responsibility for creating your program of study.

Scary word, responsibility. For all practical purposes, the attitude faculty, advisers, and academic administrators have is that students are responsible for making and living with their own academic decisions. Sure, different schools vary, often tremendously, in the amount of latitude they give students in required general education courses, required departmental courses, electives, and even curriculum choice. But the only way you can know the degree of latitude and make good choices among the alternatives is to take the responsibility to become informed. Academic decisions are only a few of the many important choices you have to make. What you should be concerned about is that you don't take things for granted—even those things you think you're pretty sure about—because it's a good bet there are a few angles you either haven't figured on or aren't aware of.

It's important that you have a good perspective on campus resources and what they can and cannot give you to help you with your academic decisions. What can you expect from your departmental adviser, the career development and placement center, the counseling center, and the like? What does it mean to "stop out" or "drop out"? How do you prepare to look for the 80% of the jobs out in the real world that never get advertised?

You need to begin by thinking about what academic advising is and what you should expect from your academic adviser. Most advisers are good at what they know, but they don't know all that you need to know to make the academic decisions that will affect you personally. This is not a failing of your adviser; it's simply a reality that there is more to academic advising than filling out a program request form. Most advisers on any campus realize that your making it through their college system can be trying at times, and it's made all the more trying by the demands put upon you by the system. Most students coming to college are obliged to declare a major or a field of concentration as incoming freshmen. But most freshmen are not ready to make that kind of commitment. About 80% of all undergraduates change their majors two to three times before they graduate, and that's not surprising. Given the wealth of choices that students have at college, it would be unusual for any incoming student to have a good handle on what he or she wants to study. Even the best high school counselors can't communicate all the opportunities that a college has to offer.

Because most of you don't have a handle on what it is you want to do, close to 50% of you will not graduate in 4 years. Even those of you who are fairly sure about what you want to do may end up taking longer to finish your degrees. You might have to stretch out school because you are working and cannot take a full semester course load. You might have personal or family problems that necessitate that you "stop out." You might have troubles dealing with the system. You might find out a bit too late that you haven't fulfilled a requirement. Or you might finally find the field of study you have been searching for, but not until the middle or end of your junior year.

Indecision is an important part of being an undergraduate, but good advising can be critical in helping you through those "decision-making blues." By admitting indecision from the start you may find yourself ahead of the game. Just talk to some of those juniors or seniors you think have it all together. You might be surprised to discover that they still have the same questions you do. Good advising can help you learn to direct your confusion into asking and answering the questions that clarify what you want.

What does this all add up to? You need to get a handle on how advising fits into the scheme of your academic life and how you can help your advisers help you. There is more to any campus than any adviser can hope to talk with you about, but with the help of advising you can learn to make college work for you. To begin, there are a few things you need to think about:

1. You can and ought to use "self-advising" as a way to take advantage of your campus.
2. What you can do on your campus is limited only by your imagination, your desire to do something with your education, your ability to ask the

right questions, and your ability to find the people who can answer those questions.

3. Don't take the prescriptions of curricula and fields of concentration for granted. Take the initiative to discover how the parts of your major fit together, how they apply to your intellectual development, your career goals, and your overall personal development and satisfaction.

Keep this in mind: Traveling is as important as arriving. By putting yourself into a community of learners you ought to be shaping an environment that gives you the best chances for enlarging yourself, exciting your intellectual curiosity, stimulating your capacity to wonder, and giving you a broader and newer perspective on the world and your place within it. Your education, then, can be the adventure it's supposed to be.

And that's the best game going.

What is good academic advising? For openers, it isn't what most people think it is—a competent bookkeeping function that tracks your progress toward graduation, or a semesterly consultation with your adviser about your next semester's course selection. In its broadest sense, academic advising should involve an assessment of your personal values, a plan for attaining intellectual fulfillment, an investigation of career direction, and a look at the "real world" from an objective and a subjective position. In a large sense it means asking "What does all this mean to me?" and learning how to go about answering that question.

Good academic advising is aimed at just that question. It's like all good educational experiences and all well-taught courses. It's a process that helps you learn to plot your path through college. It should help you orchestrate courses, resources, and other opportunities into an educational experience personally fit for you and one that seduces you into becoming personally involved in and responsible for your own learning. If your advising experience resembles something like being plugged into courses and being processed through the system in a manner akin to how your computerized forms are processed . . . it could be better.

But you know as well as we do that you aren't going to walk into very many offices on campus and find this type of advising. From the thousand times we talk to students we hear the same lines: "All our advisers do is tell us what courses we need to take. It's like a one-shot, 15-minute appointment, and they never seem interested. The whole darn place seems like it doesn't care; it's so impersonal." Right! And because you don't get everything you need in one sitting with one adviser, you take it for granted—unwarrantedly and often foolishly—that that's the way it is. Well, it isn't. You see, another line we get when we ask "Why are you taking this course?" or "Why are you in that major?" is often like "My adviser told me to take it," or "It's marketable, isn't it?" You have some kind of blind faith that what you are told to do is all there is to do, and you tend to believe what you read in the course and curriculum blurbs without taking the time to wonder if someone out there is putting one over on you. After all, if all you get from your advisers is what's written in the course catalog, why bother seeing them at all? You can read as well as they can!

The only thing you're going to get from your college programs catalog is a bare scheme of things, and its presentation will hardly tell you what you need to know. On most campuses, for instance, you can study literature through several departments such as English, Chinese, French, Russian, and comparative literature. But do any differences exist between these tracks and, if so, what? Do they offer different opportunities to utilize the resources of the campus, and is there a difference in your career marketability if you choose one track over another? For that matter, what does a person with a bachelor's in literature do? On a different line, is the best route into medical school through a traditional science? What "hidden" programs can offer you a route that is personally more attractive and offers better personal alternatives if you find you can't get into medical school? If such programs exist, how do you find out about them? You won't be able to answer these questions—if, indeed, they have even occurred to you—by consulting your college programs catalog. More important, you don't want to wait until your last year of college to begin to search out the answers.

So what do you do?

First, you need to have a sense of what advising is all about. You are the one responsible for any academic choices that affect your education. Don't take anything for granted. All that academic advisers can do, at their best, is advise from the perspective of their personal and professional experiences. But you should be aware that their professional experiences do not necessarily give them a comprehensive, overall view of your college. Departmental advisers are just that—they know about their own departments' requirements. They aren't paid to know the nooks and crannies of the campus. Still, they have their "underground networks" of people who can give them the scoop about what's going on. You can access this information, but only if you take the time to sit, talk, and ask. But you must remember that when you talk with an adviser you are consulting. Advisers are not there to tell you what to do; they are there to give you information to help you make a decision. It may not seem that way, but "advise" has a good synonym: recommend. It does not mean "command."

Second, faculty and professional advisers are not the only advisers out there. Take advantage of what parents and friends have to say, and anything else you might read, see, or hear. You cannot make a good decision until you learn how to "read" what's going on around you.

Third, for those of you at large universities, they can be big, impersonal places at first glance, and they will stay that way if you sit back and expect to bop through your degree like a "Slinky" walking down the stairs. Smaller schools can lull you into passivity, though. You need to begin to think about the difference between getting a degree and getting an education—the two are not necessarily the same. And how you pursue these options will determine whether you are a victim of the system.

Remember, if you receive inadequate services and support, most of the time it is because you haven't gone out and found out about what your college has to offer. You need to find and create your own "community"—a community of people like deans, faculty, counselors, residence hall staff, and advisers whom you can talk to on a casual and personal basis, and who can give you the inside road map to your campus. This will take time and effort, but the benefits will be worthwhile. With a good set of personal contacts you will discover that most of what you want to do academically can be done, and you can open up for yourself fields of study that are hidden beneath the surface of curricular requirements.

Finally, it's up to you to know what's going on. If you don't understand the reason for a requirement or a rule, or if you have unanswered questions, you need to ask, and you need to keep on asking until you get answers that make sense! Each college differs in how it handles rules, exceptions to rules, the substitution of courses in requirements and so on. Don't assume that you have a handle on any rule, constraint, or restriction until you check it out, and then double-check it. Many times you will find the hidden loopholes that allow department heads and deans to make exceptions to rules, and often you will find someone who will help you accomplish what you are trying to do. But you will never know for sure if you sit back passively and take college for granted. If you do, the system, with absence of malice, is going to do a number on you.

If you want to develop your relationship with faculty and get the kind of education a college can give, you have to drop one of your preconceived myths—the myth of the academic major.

From freshmen enrollment until graduation the big question put to you is "What's your major?" Let's face it, that question is one of the first things you ask when you meet someone. And if you are confused about what you're doing in school, or what you want to do with your life, you inevitably try to answer that question by finding the right major in order to put all the pieces together. When you go to career placement, the counseling center, or any other advising office, you're anxious to answer the questions: "What should I major in?" "Am I in the right major?" "I'm not happy with my major. Is there a better major for me?" And when asked about what you want to do, the answers you give always seem to revolve around "academic majors."

So you wind up in a scramble to fill in the boxes for departmental requirements, get to class, hand in required papers, and take tests. And you see faculty as those who assign papers, give you tests, and sometimes bore you to tears. Occasionally you see them to ask questions about papers, upcoming tests, or to beg for mercy. Great way to work with faculty.

Being in a major, filling the college and departmental requirements, and getting a degree are not the same as getting an education. If you want to work with faculty in a manner other than to perform the mundane tasks involved with the introductory courses they teach, the first thing you're going to have to do is learn that there may be no real educational value to the concept of academic major.

Consider this: Academic majors and departments are bureaucratic facilities. They allow colleges to house and pay faculty, and they provide compartments to place students in. They are needed to help organize areas of study and the vast numbers of students who wander through educational institutions. And, academically, they tend to reflect a common thread that runs through a variety of fields of study.

The key concept we want to emphasize is "fields of study." This is not the same as the concept of academic major. Although fields of study may be found within majors, they more closely reflect what the faculty within departments do. This is important for you to think about. To outline a field of study so that it has quality and coherence means a bit more than asking if the courses you are taking will fulfill the graduation checkoffs you need, if they will make you marketable, or if they will give you something to fall back on if all else fails. You have to change the questions you're asking and the context in which you're asking them. Being able to ask the right questions is what this ball game is about. From there it is easy to lay out how you want to answer them.

What has this to do with working with faculty? Believe it or not, how faculty approach their areas of expertise may provide a good model for you to follow, with less sophistication of course, to build a coherent education—even if you are concerned only with getting a job.

Those folks in front of your classes aren't generic political science, English, or communications professors. They are professors of political economy and resource management, literary stylistics, and legal issues in communications. They are interdisciplinary because their fields of study demand that they consider the interrelatedness of the real world. They can give you a good sense of how to put together an area of study so that the pieces of coursework you take make some sort of sense.

Consider, for instance, an interest in international relations. Sure, you might end up in the political science department. And you'll take some history and economics. But if you take your program seriously, you will have to consider that issues in international trade, East-West relations, or foreign policy cannot be studied without a foundation in ideological and religious bases for intercultural relations. Literature, art and culture, geography, and language fluency all play a critical part in developing a program sensitive to the complexities of the relations among cultures, nations, and nation-states.

For that matter, not all psych professors are psychologists. That title is generally reserved for PhDs in clinical or counseling psychology who are licensed to practice. Some social psychologists study organizational structures, integrating areas of sociology, business administration, labor relations, communications, and statistics. Brain function psychologists could just as well be working in physiology departments alongside biochemists, anatomists, and electrical engineers. Those who study attitude measurement and behavior prediction could work comfortably with political scientists, sociologists, and economists.

There may be any number of ways to approach what you want to study. It depends on your interests, how you want to orchestrate your courses, and what you feel comfortable with. But to build a field of study means to think out what it is you want to know, what it is you want to ask, and how you are going to put the pieces together. In other words, it means that you pursue an area of study in the same way that your professors do. You research the important issues, lay out what tools (courses) you need, and synthesize your solution into an undergraduate program.

The first steps, then, are to do away with the question of "What am I going to major in?" and replace it with the question "What do I want to learn and how do I want to go about it?" Doing away with the question about what you want to major in forces you to think about your education rather than letting the college programs catalog define it for you. It's at this point that you can blend your interests with what college has to offer. It's at this point that you can sit with your faculty advisers and talk with them about what it is that they do and the background they consider important. And it's at this point that you can begin to make contact with faculty in a variety of different departments who are involved with different aspects of what you are trying to build as your program of study.

You'll eventually end up declaring a major and being in a department. But how you define your major in terms of course combinations, independent study, and research agreements, and how you coordinate your extracurricular activities personalizes your major for you. It'll be a field of study that is your own and works for you.

Faculty are the moving forces of this educational establishment we've been discussing. They're the people whose brains you want to pick. You want their ideas, their commentaries on your ideas, and their advice. If you're building a field of study, faculty are the experts. Sometimes they seem to be in the ivory towers of academia, however, and don't seem very accessible. How do you find these people, and what do you say once you have located them? Some tips for the curious follow.

Timetables are academic "Sears Catalogs." Small gems and good bargains are frequently hidden in obscure places. Faculty teach under their departmental sponsorship, even if their course titles are far afield from their departments' major focuses. International relations may be a "natural" for a political science department, but at one school we know, a former ambassador has an appointment in the sociology department. By carefully looking through all course offerings, new possibilities may surface.

Faculty show off their true interests in upper-level courses and in special-topics seminars. Departments go potluck when assigning instructors to introductory courses, so if you want to know who specializes in specific areas, look at upper-division and graduate level offerings. Keep a special eye out for seminar courses, too.

Although you may not take these courses, you have located your specialists here. And if you can't get into these courses for credit, you may be able to sit in. But, more important, you will find faculty expertise and crossdisciplinary interests in these courses. For instance, when you discover the course in geography of world conflict, international relations begins to take on a different bent, especially if your interest is national security policy. This, when tied to special-topics courses in communications, physics, and economics, begins to make a field of study.

At this point you need to do a few things.

Contact the professors of these courses to talk over what your interests are and what you hope to gain from their courses. Get their current course descriptions and look over their reading lists. Find out from these professors who else they know who are doing things in your areas of interest.

Many departments publish listings of their faculty's interests. At larger schools, these lists are often part of the promotional package for prospective graduate students. Ask the departmental secretary for this information. That person usually knows more than most students realize!

Check out all upcoming seminars and lectures. Go to some of these in your areas of interest. You'll usually hear an informative talk and find out who on campus is involved in these areas.

Once you begin to get a sense of who's doing what, think about how it fits in with what you want to do. Then, either get on the phone to make appointments with people, or see them during office hours. You need to talk with faculty about how to make your program of study substantive. And you need to talk to them about a few more things. You need to find out if there are ongoing groups of people (faculty and students alike) who meet to discuss the things you care about. They may be meeting through any one of the study groups on campus. Sure, you may not be able to participate in some of these groups. On the other hand, you can find out who members are and what the possibilities are of doing independent study with them. And there is nothing to stop a faculty member from inviting you to these seminars.

Make use of your elective hours to get into special-topics courses you've located, create special-topics courses with the faculty you've discovered, or convince faculty to do independent study with you. Here's where real education takes place. In these courses you will be asked to think, apply the tools you have learned, and produce your own work. Faculty usually are willing to teach under such arrangements as long as they know you're serious.

Find out about ongoing research projects in your areas of interest. Try tying into these projects. If the people on these projects feel you're energetic, want to learn, and can contribute through good efforts, they'll listen to you. Faculty won't usually turn away good help. Here's an approach that seems to work: "Professor B., I've been reading some of your articles on international economic development in Latin America. I'm interested in your theory on the interaction of cultural patterns and economic growth. I'd like to work on this problem with you." If you tie into ongoing research projects or independent study, you learn how people define the critical problems in their areas, how they learn to ask the right questions to find solutions to those problems, and what it takes to come up with workable answers. And that's what you're going to have to do when you get out of college—regardless of your field.

But keep this in mind—you cannot do any of these things in a vacuum. You have to integrate the things you already know into your educational plan. You also have to increase the amount of information you get and learn to think about how it pertains to you. You have to start listening to information radio, like "Morning Edition" and "All Things Considered," on National Public Radio. You also have to read major national newspapers and magazines. And how about trade journals and papers that the professionals read? Don't wait till senior year to do this. Even if you're a freshman, do it now.

Education versus training. We've heard this tossed around quite a lot recently. We've heard faculty, deans, and top-level administrators cry about what they see as the single-minded, narrowly viewed pursuit of vocationalism among students. They claim that too many of you come to college to be trained to get jobs and sacrifice your chances for real "liberal learning." And if the students we've talked to are any indication, the faculty may be right. After all, there are only so many times we can sit and listen to students ask us how to get into a major that is going to bring in a lot of cash. But more disturbing is the trend we see developing toward minimal competency—almost functional illiteracy. Many of the students we talk with simply can't think critically, logically, or in an orderly way. Nor do they want to. They only want what it takes to land them a job.

But then we've also heard students ask why they should care about what the difference is between education and training. After all, look at the education they seem to be getting at college. Students are not encouraged to interact in their courses or with faculty. They've been told too many times that large universities are research institutions, or they have seen good teachers at small liberal arts colleges canned because they didn't publish enough to get tenure. Faculty, they feel, have to research first and teach maybe third. As in high school, students are put into courses implicitly to be respondents, to absorb. They aren't asked too many times to use their heads in class or to work creatively with course content. That would require some effort from their teachers and take them away from their primary tasks of research and publication. If the administration gave anything more than lip service to their rhetoric about education and learning, there would be some substantive changes in teaching, advising, and other support services. Students may be right about this.

One thing is sure—it's risky looking for a rewarding education that depends on accidental excellence.

Let's get one thing aired first. Virtually everyone in college is out to get jobs. Even doctoral candidates in philosophy, comparative literature, and music history do not pursue their education simply for the love of wisdom. They do so to become trained professionals in their fields. And all the faculty who float their credentials for offers of better positions or as bargaining chips are doing it for the money, the position, and upward mobility. Much the same is true for many administrators—for instance, deans need a dean's position to apply for chancellorships. If they weren't concerned with career advancement, they'd just have library cards, pursue their studies as recreation, and work wherever. They're just as vocationally oriented as any undergrad pursuing an accounting major. The difference is that their marketplace is not the commercial world—it's the academic world.

What's the issue then?

Some of us, many of us maybe, are bothered that students seem to be becoming as compartmentalized as their various general education requirements and as

31

isolated as their core curricula are isolated from other majors. Many students are bothered by this also. The panacea prescribed for this, the panacea that is supposed to offset the effects of vocationalism and the narrowly specialized curricula, is to encourage—or demand—students to pursue liberal education requirements in order to foster a sense of values, a sense of shared history, and, as some have said, to bind us together as a society.

Nice, fashionable idea. But don't bet that if you take a few humanities courses you're going to be better off, or that exposure to something is better than nothing. The idea of a liberal education is not so much in course content or the ability to pull out a neat quote as it is in acquiring the intellectual skills and abilities to develop conceptual sophistication and critical judgment. And that can come from any field of study.

Each domain has its established ways of inquiry, its ways of looking at the world and making sense of it. It's this functional similarity among fields of study you should be concerned with. This means simply that nothing inherent in any program on campus makes it vocational or not, and nothing makes one program inherently better than another at churning out so-called "liberally educated" people. The key is how you pursue your learning. Just because you know a few historical facts, can tell somebody that you've read Shakespeare, or have taken a foreign language doesn't mean you have a claim on liberal education. And more important, majoring in any of the traditional liberal arts majors gives you no claim to being critically insightful, aesthetically appreciative, or morally responsible. Enough has been said on this to question whether any liberal arts program can ensure that students will develop intellectual curiosity and powers of reason.

This is not a pitch to say that because you want to graduate and get a good job that something is wrong with you. Hey—we want to get good jobs ourselves! What you need to understand is that the faculty and administration are telling you that you can get a liberal education and also be marketable. And in fact, what they know and may not be getting across to you is that by trying to combine both, you may be more marketable and more satisfied with what you are trying to do with your lives.

You can't do this by banking on either courses or a major to do it for you. You have to do it for yourselves. It's how you approach school and put together general education requirements, electives, and your major so they hang together in some personal sense that allows you to grow professionally, grapple with the ethical complexities of living with people, and look at the significance of your own life.

You've got to fill general ed and elective hours. They can be "stinking requirements" to get out of the way as quickly, easily, and vacantly as possible. Or, because you have to take them anyway, you could make this all work for you. You could build a coherent and personally satisfying education. What you might find out is that learning, especially learning how to learn, can be fun. And you can still be marketable!

CHAPTER 4

MAKING RESOURCES VISIBLE

Colleges are learning resources—assemblages of people, books, and laboratories—and environments of things, ideas, passions, and ideals. Campus advice givers play a critical role in helping students orchestrate these resources to harmonize with their individual personal and educational goals. Advice givers can help create an atmosphere of collegiality and cooperation among those areas of the campus that address research, teaching, student development, and academic advising. Advice givers must also help students understand and see the interrelations among these areas. These resources and their interrelationships are often as invisible to advice givers as they are to students. This chapter will illustrate how these resources and interrelationships can be made more visible and viable to advice givers in their task of helping students understand the workings of their campuses.

This process does not require the creation of a different administrative structure nor a major change in academic advising systems. It simply requires a shift in attitude and approach and a shift in how advice givers help students access campus resources. Advice givers need to help students learn to see colleges in terms of functional intersections instead of structural roadblocks.

APPROPRIATE REFERRALS

Students often need help to get to the person who can interpret rules and requirements properly. As obvious as this seems, it is often the obvious that is overlooked. Rules are not, nor should they be, strictures that invariably limit what can and cannot be done on a campus. For example, many colleges have "drop deadlines," the last permissible day for dropping courses without penalty. Without conferring with the proper campus authority, students may assume that these dates are nonnegotiable. They may not know that viable excuses, such as documented health or psychological problems, or borderline class performance are sometimes acceptable rationales for extending the deadlines.

Many systems are geared to give students a chance, without penalty, to make class progress under normal conditions. Sometimes the right person can help students "bend" the rules if what they are trying to accomplish makes good educational sense. Students may find that what they thought they could not do can be done another way. Students may also learn, through this process, that what they thought was a ridiculous restriction really has a well-thought out and reasonable rationale. In this way, they learn about their relationships to the larger system of their colleges rather than simply looking at rules from an egocentric perspective.

THE PROBLEM: INVISIBLE RESOURCES

Advice givers can play a key role in making resources visible. For instance, curricula often cannot keep pace with advances in fields of study, changes in the work place, and new ideas and technologies in the work world. Faculty, however, attempt to keep pace. But finding appropriate faculty may be as difficult for advice givers as it is for students. Faculty research is often "invisible" to advice givers and students alike because it does not ordinarily take place in undergraduate courses and faculty advising.

Advice givers can help students coordinate their use of a variety of campus experts. For instance, advice givers can teach students how to use career guidance specialists, working professionals, and reference librarians to investigate how career possibilities and personal interests fit into the fields of study students are trying to construct.

THE PROBLEM: CREATING NETWORKS

In order to direct students in their first steps toward accessing hidden resources, advice givers need to have a network informing them of ongoing faculty and campus professionals' research and expertise. Without such a network, advice givers can only guess at the diversity of expertise and interests that exists on campus.

For instance, one faculty member we know is an important referral for students who wish to pursue studies in East-West relations and arms control. We discovered, in a passing conversation, that this individual also had an active interest in maritime law and would be a useful resource for those wishing to study trade relations among Commonwealth nations and the United States.

The frequent disparity between faculty members' titles and their interests is another problem. Many members of the campus community have active interests in areas that are quite different from what their professorial titles indicate. For instance, a dean of students we know is also an opera aficionado. His recreational interests, blended with his professional expertise, make him a reliable referral for students wishing to study arts administration. This illustration is more common than not.

A student affairs professional at a small liberal arts school, for example, has interests in sports history. He is also a published sports journalist. He finds himself playing an active academic role with students both as an adviser and as a director of independent study in sports and society.

Consider a professor of industrial engineering who is politically involved in local health policy making. She helps students realize how work in operations research can be a key element in health policy and administration studies

Campus phone directories abound with a wealth of people, many outside the mainstream of campus educational life, who can contribute to educational life. The director of business affairs, chief development officer, campus legal counsel, director of campus recreation, and director of housing are all resources. They are people students can talk with about aspects of their educational plans, developing trends, and internship opportunities. Clearly, matching faculty and administrators' interests with educational opportunities for undergraduates must be based on something more than passing conversations.

THE SOLUTION: TAKING THE INITIATIVE ON CAMPUS

Advice givers must actively contribute to a collaborative effort that blends research, teaching, student development, and advising into a cooperative educational venture. Often, when advice givers take the initiative, the results of their efforts help campus colleagues get a better handle on what their fellows are engaged in and their own college resources. In turn, the results of these efforts provide a base for students to find the learning resources that make up colleges.

Initiatives

1. *Create faculty/staff research and professional interest guides.* Directories of this type can be as simple as alphabetized lists of faculty and staff by department that include statements of each person's current research objectives, professional and ancillary interests, current consulting activities, latest papers presented, publications, book and grant reviews, outside professional activities, and places where graduate study was done. The object is to create a catalog that will promote an understanding of the diversity of faculty and staff expertise and interests and to provide a guide to match their interests with the educational interests of undergraduates. This is a relatively simple task, easily accomplished on a standard personal computer. Yet the effect of this collation can be significant. A project of this kind also can affect collaboration within and between various disciplines and can provide an opportunity to match faculty and staff interests with research and teaching support.

2. *Gain a good understanding of library resources, and work cooperatively with reference librarians.* Our experience has shown that reference librarians are seldom stumped. They can give advice givers and students invaluable resources, no matter how "off the wall" their questions may seem to be. Advice givers with access to a comprehensive research library have the benefit of librarians with indexes, books, and journals right at hand. Advice givers at smaller schools will find that reference librarians usually have access to indexes, and they can access most materials through interlibrary loans.

Libraries also provide advice givers and students a means for learning about faculty research. Faculty write books and articles that contribute to the substance of the academic fields students study. Many of their works are similar to the texts and articles that students are required to read for their classes. By "researching" their faculty, students can see faculty's interests and how those interests may fit in with their own educational plans. More important, students and faculty can find common ground to begin talking about a field of study. Again, the nature of the library becomes an issue. Comprehensive research libraries will generally have the books and journals where faculty work can be found. Advice givers at smaller schools can take the initiative to work with reference librarians to create a "faculty browsing library," a section in the library devoted to books, published papers, conference papers, working papers, and other works by their own faculty. The effect of this is to bring faculty research into the students' learning environment.

3. *Become familiar with the laboratories, departmental facilities, centers for faculty area studies or interdisciplinary studies, ongoing colloquia and lecture*

36

series, college and university art museums, performing arts facilities, student and faculty literary magazines, campus radio and newspapers, and campus public information services. Advice givers also need to encourage students to become familiar with these resources. These, and more, make up an integral part of the academic life or a campus. These resources afford a perspective on how theory is turned into practice and a sense that what goes on in the academic realm does have an impact on the outside world. Advice givers can show students how these facilities provide possibilities for independent study and internships.

4. *Read college timetables thoroughly and teach students how to read them.* This may not be as obvious as it seems. Advice givers need to familiarize themselves with the procedural matters outlined in the timetables. They also need to take the time to scan all the course offerings. Even at mul-tiuniversities this task can be accomplished in half an hour. Courses that would be beneficial to students are sometimes listed in places where students normally would not look. For instance, a student studying in-ternational relations might find a course in the geography of world conflict listed under geography, not under the more obvious departments of history or political science. Many students, especially freshmen and sophomores, are hindered by what might be called "timetable blinders." They tend to look at the courses for which they feel their "year" in college has readied them. It seldom occurs to students that by looking at the topics of senior seminars, special-topics seminars, or graduate level seminars they may gain insight into who the faculty are and the various fields of study in which faculty are engaged. By sitting in on seminars, students may get a sense of a field and may identify potential faculty mentors. Advice givers and students, then, need to understand that timetables offer more than course listings.

5. *Teach students how to better "read," "listen," and "view" what is going on around them.* Advice givers need to encourage students to expand their range by broadening the quantity and quality of the information they receive. Many students are unfamiliar with popular information sources such as *The New York Times*, National Public Radio, or public television. Most students do not realize that many of the things they read, hear, and see in the popular media can contribute to fields of study and may be interests of one the faculty on their campus. Few students realize that virtually every profession has its own "trade paper" or journal that can provide valuable insight into the "who," "what," and "where" of that profession. Advice givers can help students by showing them how to "read" about their personal issues in the media and how to connect those issues with college resources.

These are by no means all of the ways advice givers can begin to make resources visible and create networks for students. Advice givers have to challenge the roles they have traditionally played. They can and should play a critical integrative role, one that makes the educational resources of a school as visible and accessible as possible.

ESSAYS ON ACCESSING AND UNDERSTANDING FACULTY AND OTHER CAMPUS RESOURCES

The essays in this section explain how students can access faculty, other campus professionals, and campus resources. The first essay is instructive, illustrating where students should go for help regarding rules and academic concerns. The second, third, and fourth essays are informative. They discuss the faculty's role on campus, a generalized description of the generation gap between students and faculty/staff, and the role of college instructors as teachers. These essays lay the foundation for understanding the basic differences between high school and college teaching. They also provide insights into how college teachers approach their work and their students. The fifth essay is written from a developmental viewpoint and suggests academic strategies for dealing with each of the 4 years of college. The sixth essay is confrontational. It represents a cynical view of students that faculty and student affairs professionals express when they hit the low points in the semester. This essay is included to illustrate to students the other side of the coin—when faculty get discouraged. It is meant to raise eyebrows and get people to rethink their positions. This information can be directly passed to students, can be used as the basis of programs and group discussions, and can be incorporated into advice-giving strategies.

Course selection time! Scramble that timetable! Get a good schedule!

Most campuses have a midsemester advising period with a name like "advance enrollment," a time when you drop by your department, chat with your adviser, drop off your course request forms, and amble away into the sunset. So much for advance enrollment.

This is the way it should be if your have already reviewed your academic condition, have a good sense of your progress toward a degree, have met with your adviser to look at the fine points of your field of study, and have plotted out different course groupings to see how the pieces fit together.

But if advance enrollment is the once-over through the timetable and a drop-off of your course requests on your way to lunch, then you might be headed into a college wasteland or, possibly, a mediocre education.

Two different issues emerge here—rules and academic concerns. You need to know whom you can trust in each of these areas. Those who are good at rules might not be good with academic concerns. It may be as simple as someone who can give you the right referral on the first round or someone who can interpret and "bend" rules in your behalf.

Every campus differs as to which members of the faculty and administration hold important powers and abilities. It's important for you to identify these people so you know where to seek help when you need it. What's equally important is knowing when you need help. Some rules of thumb follow.

Someone is the ultimate authority on rules. For academic issues on many campuses, that person has a title like academic dean. On other campuses, a department chair may be your head honcho. For nonacademic issues, it's someone like the dean of students. Their jobs are to administer policy. What they tell you is "right," and right or wrong, it stands. But they are also your primary sources on how exceptions to the rules can be made. They aren't out to get you, and if what you want to do makes sense, you will find some of them more than willing to work with you. That's right! These people can be your friends. One tip: Administrators aren't elephants; they forget. If you're working on an exception to a rule or on extensions on a deadline, make sure you get it in writing.

Some office personnel also interpret rules. These people translate every course you take into what counts toward graduation, toward your major, and what courses transfer from other schools. They keep track of employer interviews and financial aid, too. They know policies. And if they aren't sure about a policy they should know that, too! But they usually know how to ask for the answers. You ought to check with your records keepers once in a while to get the scoop on your academic progress. The official records will confirm what you think you've accomplished. You transfer students should be especially alert to checking on your status.

Professional advisers, who are mainly large campus phenomena, sit in between administrative and academic concerns. Most aren't scholars in the fields they advise; they are hired by departments to devote time and energy to advising procedures. They have a good grasp of their departments' and colleges' rules and academic requirements. But most are not expected to be involved in the nitty-gritty of the different academic areas that make up their departments. They are expected to give you good referrals to departmental faculty.

Faculty are experts in their academic areas. They are not necessarily hired to advise you on nuts-and-bolts procedures. If you are interested in the differences between biomechanics and exercise physiology or what operations research is, faculty can tell you. But you also need to keep in mind that they may not speak at the general level you need. Get second, third, and fourth opinions, and put together your own story. If you run into faculty who can also help you interpret rules and look at the academic implications of your choices, you're home free.

Graduate students (your teaching assistants—TAs), another large campus phenomenon, are "novice faculty." Most are fairly knowledgeable and currently up on their fields. They know where many of the new trends are and where their fields are going. They have recently finished the first round of the paper chase and the grad school application process. They should have a sense of the national picture of who is doing what in their fields and what those fields are looking for in terms of undergraduate preparation. And, they are fairly easy to talk to. But beware: They do not know the rules unless they have been hired and oriented as advisers. (If you're on an undergraduate campus, you won't find grad students unless you go on a road trip to a university. It may well be worth your while.)

Your buddies all have their opinions and at least one backup story, but it's risky to act on their advice without checking it out. Everyone, for instance, knows someone who got out of a language requirement. But what they might not know or fail to tell you is that that someone perforated his ear drums with popsicle sticks and still had to plead his case for 3 years before his petition was approved. Your buddies haven't been at college much longer than you so don't count on their having the inside lines to all that you can do on campus. But if they are out there looking and asking, they might be finding some leads and turning up things you haven't. Remember, what may sound crazy to your buddies may make a whole lot of sense for you.

The reference librarians can be your unsung heroes and heroines. You usually think of the library as a place to study, to get books and articles, and to pick up dates. But the library has a wealth of information that is important to you and that the reference librarian can help you get. For instance, the reference librarian helped a student to identify those corporations that only did business between France and Chicago. By being directed to the right index this student saved hours of frustration and was able to use that information to negotiate internships in both Chicago and Paris. These librarians are hard to stump. So if you're wondering "How do I find out about X?" talk with your reference librarian.

And don't forget the local recreational facility or gym. Crazy? Maybe. But that "old guy" who just trounced you on the racketball court or that "older woman" who blew you off the track is probably faculty or staff. Just as the TV commercials suggest, some of the best campus connections are made in the locker room. But instead of pushing sweat-free underarms, we're pushing information exchange. Free—no sweat. Remember, when you're talking with these folks about their sports, you're talking on a people level. Does this lead you to believe that you might be able to talk with them on a people level about other things as well?

We've left out bunches of people who can give good advice: counseling psychologists, career placement counselors, and paraprofessional peers to name a few. And there is more that you can do.

Visit courses you plan to take. Few profs object to visitors in their classes. You can get a handle on the course content and style of your potential instructors. Take time to find the people who will be teaching the courses you plan to take and talk to them about why you will be taking their courses. Sometimes you may find that what's in the course description is not what is going to be taught or that the course is not going to add to your program what you thought it would. Often the instructor can clue you in on some useful alternatives.

Scan the bookstore. You not only get a handle on the reading lists of the courses you're taking but also get a sense of what sorts of reading material will be used in other courses. From the books on the shelves, you might find yourself running into a few courses you would not normally think of as important to you.

Pay attention to the dates on the college catalog and handbooks you use. The dates on these books are not for kicks. Requirements change from time to time. You are governed by the documents that are dated at the time you first entered. Many students have fouled up their progress toward a degree because the books they were following applied to a different entering freshman class. These books are sometimes confusing and sometimes written in a strange administrative language. If you have any questions, be sure to ask, because nobody is going to come knocking on your door.

It's up to you to ask questions and get answers. If you put in some legwork, ask some questions, and do some planning, you can have your campus at your feet.

College students are a special breed. For some reason, you decided to keep at the books for 4 more years. The past 12 years weren't enough, huh? If you've gotten this far, some people would say you're smart. Who knows? What you've shown, though, is that you're pretty adept at "doing school." And college is just the next natural step.

After being on campus for a while you come to feel you're involved with the college community: You're active in social organizations, intramural sports, and student government. You have guessed pretty well that much of your "real learning" comes outside the classroom. You probably think that a large part of a good education has to do with gaining maturity, responsibility, and the ability to relate to different people, including your peers.

There's school, of course, but that's doing homework, writing some papers, and studying for tests. You're good at these tasks. They are almost routine— your college boards tell us you can do them well. But the concept of intellectual development doesn't seem to be in your view of what college is all about.

It's not hard to figure where you want all this to lead—a degree that will buy you a future. Most of you aren't at college to prepare for graduate study, and most of us know that. You get into school, make out, and get out. And most of us expect you to fit this profile because most of us were the same way as undergrads.

So, how come so many of us campus types have a hard time talking with you? And how come so many of you feel it's so hard to talk with us? Well, as much as we don't like to admit it—especially after many of us swore it would never happen—the old generation gap is raising its head. It might not be a bad idea to let you folks know what we mean by this.

Most faculty and most of the other folks their age with whom you come into contact on campus were forced to confront a myriad of social and political issues during their years in undergrad and graduate school—several wars and major protests; civil rights, freedom riders, and voting rights; women's and minority access to education, jobs, and housing; a major confrontation with honesty in the federal government, Joe McCarthy, Watergate, and Nixon's resignation; the advent of nuclear energy and the bomb. To them, the Beatles aren't Paul McCartney's old band and Bob Dylan wrote lyrics that people pondered in term papers. And some of Jerry Garcia's peers are now tenured faculty, deans of students, and directors of housing who took the *Electric Kool Aid Acid Test* 20 years ago.

The people who are teaching you have been weaned in an environment of social and political activism. Some of them became active because they had to. The issues included much more than the protest against the Vietnam War. Much that the people of that era worked for and brought about has a direct effect on the health and well-being on your campus. The issues they have confronted in their own professional development and advancement have given you the 18-year-old vote, the end of the draft, desegregation, women's rights, equal access, affirmative action, and Title IX. They helped bring students onto university committees, encouraged and ensured admission of women into business and engineering majors, and freed you from parental restrictions that governed student life. They helped bring about coed residence halls, eradication of 10:30 p.m. "hours," and 24-hour visitation. And keep in mind, most of these are fairly recent happenings.

It wasn't that most of these folks were unduly idealistic or even revolutionary. They weren't out there forsaking jobs and economic security for a cause. In many cases it was the opposite. Remember, the economy was different, and when most of your faculty were finishing their bachelor's, a college degree was a carte blanche passport into a wide-open job market. Their generation could surpass their parents' level of affluence. (You, as a generation, may not be able to expect this.)

It was one thing for a man to come out of college with an education, a degree, and a job. Things were altogether different for women. They found out that they got paid 17% less for the same jobs and were "hit on" in the bargain because they looked good in skirts. Because they were looking for good educations and good jobs but wanted to be treated equally, with respect and humanity, women found themselves faced with the fact that they had to fight. Many women became feminists not for ideological reasons but because workaday realities forced it upon them.

The end result is that many faculty tend to be sensitive to social/political issues because they've been taught, often the hard way, that what may not look immediately important can have critical, sometimes adverse, consequences on personal futures.

So campuses today resemble two rams butting their heads against each other. Many of you are here looking to acquire specific skills, get a good job, and look out for number one. The faculty are trying to tell you there's more to it. You can get those specific skills and get a good job. But there's more you can do with your learning. You can also use your education to help learn how to look out for others around you, to learn how to care and lend a hand, and in doing so you may find out something rather interesting—you enhance the quality of your own life by helping to enhance the quality of everything around you. By looking out for others, you end up really looking out for number one.

"Publish or perish;" "Up or out." That's the name of the game for faculty, the bottom line. It's surprising how many of you students don't know what these phrases mean. If you don't, you might be blind to the effect this reality has on your education.

Faculty at 4-year colleges and universities are hired to be scholars. Sure, the job listings ask for someone to handle courses in modern European history, organizational policy, or solid state physics. But teaching is only one aspect of what faculty are hired to do. They are expected to do many tasks, but generating original, high-quality contributions to their fields of study is a first priority. Research, publishing, presenting papers, and bringing in grant money are the concerns of faculty at many colleges. This doesn't mean that they don't like to teach, or that they don't like to work with students, or that they won't try to do a good job at both. It means that under the agenda governing them, teaching and advising are not always first priorities.

Here's the basic scheme.

Assistant professors are on the tenure-track treadmill. They have about 7 years to produce enough research, conference papers, articles, chapters in books, books, and grants to have a shot at tenure; and tenure is important. It's lifetime job security! To boot, they also need to gain regional and national recognition, contribute to department and college committees, and be captains of their departmental softball teams. About 3 years into this run they are reviewed to see if their "progress" is sufficient. At the 7-year review they are given tenure and usually a promotion to associate professor. Or they are "let go." Assistant professors are in a pressure cooker.

Associate professors feel the pressure too. For their promotions to full professors they are judged on further criteria of high-powered scholarship: the stature of the journals and presses in which their articles and books are published; the status of the conferences where their papers are presented; the frequency with which their work is cited by others in their field; opinions of their national and international colleagues; and the amount of grant money they generate.

This isn't the total picture by any means. This isn't high school, where teachers are hired to be teachers. Publications and research in major journals bring your college prestige. Major grants enable the college to be a place where important research is conducted (not to mention the 50% to 67% that is figured into each grant as overhead charges, which go directly into the school's general operating budget). Outside consulting signifies that faculty make important national and international contributions. These are some of the status-getting factors that go into ranking schools—publications, successful grant-getting, and recognition by peers. Never underestimate the institution's quest for status. It generates more and better grants, higher quality faculty, more alumni gifts, and a reputation that attracts more undergraduate admissions applications. Let's face it: Money, prestige, and education are a menage a trois that is hard to separate.

Conspicuously absent from this scheme is teaching and advising. In tenure decisions good teaching does carry some weight—not much—but it can tip the scale in some instances. How heavily these two tasks are weighted depends on the individual college's philosophy. But if the research and publications aren't there, no matter how good a teacher an assistant professor may be, at many colleges that person is headed for the door. And make no doubt about it—tenure is sought with a vengeance. And advising . . . well it usually doesn't generate many points.

This doesn't mean that faculty do not take teaching and advising seriously. As in other professional activities, they have a genuine concern for doing quality work. They do have egos, you know. And a genuine case can be made that quality instruction is best had from scholars who are on the forefront of their areas of expertise. But faculty have to do a balancing act, with teaching and advising being only two of many factors to weigh. When other factors carry more weight in the tenure/promotion scheme, and when faculty may want to take time to play a game of catch with the kids, where would you put your cookies?

On a university campus there is also the issue of "divided attention." Most professors teach graduate level courses and direct graduate students' research. Working with more advanced students at upper-division levels fulfills much of these faculty's spiritual and temporal obligations to teaching and advising. Undergraduates are on the bottom of the pile in these situations. Faculty who are successful in their research frequently become "released" from undergraduate teaching and advising to devote more time to research and graduate instruction.

So what does this mean to an undergraduate?

Next time you can't find your professors or faculty advisers, you can bet they aren't watching "General Hospital." But remember this—you can create some wonderful working relationships, and sometimes personal friendships, with faculty. Despite the pressures and constraints on their time, faculty generally enjoy working with students. After all, that's one of the reasons they got into this racket. Given you now know some of the basic rules of the game, make it work for you.

You've all had at least one teacher you've considered great, someone who got you genuinely excited about learning. But what makes a good teacher? First, consider the difference between teaching in high school and teaching in college.

In general, high school teachers impart information to help students make sense of the world. Prominent among these teachers' aims is to teach skills and impart community values so that students can operate above a merely functional level in society. One hopes that these teachers also instill an excitement for learning and critical thinking and help their students become responsible and independent members of society.

The difference between college and high school teachers is significant. In addition to being teachers, college professors are active scholars who are engaged in challenging the given "truths" of fields of study. Anytime people question the givens of a knowledge base they are in a position to advocate change. One role of colleges and universities in society, then, is to promote change, and most scholars at these schools take the position that absolutes don't exist. All concepts should be challenged, modified, or done away with as they lose their ability to account for an increasing awareness of the complexity of human experience. In this sense, colleges have the role of challenging the status quo. Consequently, college teaching can be a type of subversive activity.

The average freshman comes to college believing in absolutes . . . either it is or it isn't . . . it's right or wrong. But college teaching works in a relativistic framework. College teacher/scholars do not teach to confirm student perceptions. They aren't necessarily advocating that you change your perceptions, but they should be challenging you to develop analytic skills either to confirm, revise, or reject the ideas you hold.

If higher education were only to teach about and reaffirm the status quo, it would be at odds with its own nature. The roles of the teacher/scholar, as well as the psychologist, career counselor, and residence hall director, are to push you beyond what you know. This should both scare and excite you. These people are the wilderness guides of your minds. You have to trust them and doubt them at the same time. Good college teachers push their students into the unknown, teach them to search, to doubt, to question, to analyze, and to interpret. They communicate through the various methodologies that make up their fields and through their intellectual views of reality. This is not what most undergraduates expect. Undergraduates tend to act from the gut. Before college is over, students should be integrating their heads into this process.

But what makes a good teacher? Intent is not enough. Perhaps 90% of all college professors have never taken a course in teaching methodology, let alone the theory of testing and measurement. They wing it from day one. Some do well, most are okay, and some flounder helplessly. They're hired to be scholars, and for the most part they are rewarded for the nonteaching parts of their academic activities. What makes a good researcher is one thing; what makes a good teacher/scholar is another.

Style and commitment are essential. But informal interviews with those professors who have consistently received top awards for undergraduate teaching reveal many other important ingredients. The bottom line is a genuine interest in what they do and in their students. These faculty care, and their students know it. Even if they teach in large, impersonal lecture hall settings, their caring comes through. As teacher/scholars, these profs are all actively involved in and committed to their academic fields. They involve their students in their excitement. Some are viewed as great "entertainers," others as "heavy thinkers." Their styles differ, but their ability to incorporate into their teaching methods an excitement about what they do seems to be a critical factor. They treat students not as information receptacles, paper writers, and test takers, but as people like themselves, and as people who are about to discover the thrill of their classes. These instructors teach to transfer that thrill. They identify with student needs and communicate their ideas within a framework students understand. They sense when they're not getting through and then modify their approach. They also involve their students, not as empty containers to be filled with words of wisdom, but as actively engaged novice-scholars.

Because college teachers tend to be area specialists, you need to recognize the circumstances that best reflect their teaching strengths. Some of the people who are said to be the better undergraduate teachers are really not active "frontier" scholars. Most are experts in their fields and have made solid contributions; when you get them on a roll about their specialties, they're dynamic. They have made specific efforts to develop teaching styles that work and that convey interest and excitement about their areas of study. And then there are the heavies. They are not simply experts in their specialties. They have made contributions to their fields that have shaped the foundations and directions of their areas of study. They not only have overviews of their fields but also a sense of where their fields will be going in the future, because they are the ones making that future.

What underlies how well all these people teach is how they tie the parts of their discipline into coherent wholes and how they create this coherency before your eyes and ears. They present their models for cogent thinking, entice you into this process, and help you incorporate what makes sense to you into your own intellectual repertoires. If you combine this with their challenge to you to submit your ideas to their critical minds, you can learn how to learn, how to think critically, and how to open yourselves to what makes education exciting.

Each of your 4 years of college can be characterized by a set of issues that you confront as you become more familiar with the environment, become committed to a field of study, learn about yourselves and your relationships to others, and become actively involved with your lifelong learning process and career definitions. Most people don't recognize their issues and merely ride through these years, developing fantastic yearly hindsights and great "If I only had . . ." statements. Although these scenarios may not fit you personally, maybe the scenes we portray will get your cogs turning and springs winding.

Freshman year is not under your control. You declare a major or don't declare a major, and someone tells you what to do in accordance with how you categorize yourself. And how you categorize yourself may or may not have any relationship to your freshman year realities. Freshman year can be characterized as a time when you learn a lot about yourself and about your relationship to others. Whether you get heavily into academics—which is different from "doing homework"— is doubtful. Your freshman year is probably built on your total trust of some adviser or catalog. From now on, though, it's your ball game and you are the manager of your own team.

For those of you getting ready to jump into sophomore year, you need to get a handle on your educational goals. You can usually sit undecided until this year is over, but then the pressure is on to declare a major. Sophomore year is a good time to construct a course-selection strategy that leads you in several potential directions and that lets you check out options you think may be attractive. Think through how you want your education to progress. Thumb through your time-table, look at the upper-level courses in the areas you're considering, and build a schedule that lets you get a handle on what makes up the fields of study that may interest you.

A shotgun blast of introductory courses won't give you a good idea about how various fields of study are put together. These introductory courses are hardly more than cursory surveys. One positive strategy is to pick a broad area of study that uses several approaches. Explore how related courses interconnect and also explore how each course can lead in its own direction. Economics, for instance, can be readily explored at the sophomore level for social issues (women in the labor market), quantitative methods common to many areas of research and analysis (statistics), international issues and political implications (comparative economic systems, international economics, or comparative political systems), marketing implications (the family as a consumer unit), and governmental roles (public finance or government regulation of economic activity). You are looking for how the course content and methodologies fit your interests and abilities, not whether the course was interesting or boring. Teachers make courses interesting or boring. That's not the issue in this strategy.

Another strategy is to take courses that present interdisciplinary approaches. Courses with titles like Foundations of American Education look at the institution of school from social, philosophical, historical, psychological, political, and economic perspectives. The Contemporary World: Political, Ideological, and International Forces presents another interdisciplinary approach.

Without seriously looking into relationships between courses and how these courses fit into the big picture, you might still flounder through your sophomore year.

For those of you entering junior year, think about the substantive content of your field of study. You have 2 more years to put together fundamental and supporting courses, independent study, and internships to build a strong educational program. If you're thinking more about how to get those last 10 courses to fulfill your degree requirements and some electives for fillers, you may not be using your time wisely. Look for coherence, a scheme that will fit the pieces of your studies into an educational theme that pleases you. The idea here is that your field of study may not be isolated from other fields of study. International trade, for instance, considers how language, culture, and history can make a significant difference in how you might study trade relations with other countries. These studies complement an international relations field of study but are not readily identified as such in the catalog.

Finally, for those of you entering senior year, now is the time to put the icing on the cake. This is the year you want to contract for independent study work, cement relations with faculty, line up your on-campus internships, and add those extra pieces to make your program strong. Use this last year to give you a level of expertise consistent with your area of study, which can give you a jump on the next steps once you graduate. Plan a year of study that helps you confront the difficult tasks of making interpretive decisions and consider the implications of those decisions. At this point, it's not cumulative exposure to subject matter you should be after, but learning how to think critically.

Keep these thoughts in the back of your mind. To become an educated person involves more than just taking a coherent set of courses. You must also nurture your capacity to make informed and responsible moral choices. A historical understanding can help you better recognize the complexity, ambiguity, and uncertainty in human affairs of which you'll be a part. Use your general education courses and those extra electives wisely. They can make the qualitative difference between being trained and being educated.

Yes, there's a generation gap between students and many of the faculty. Perhaps this is because many of the issues you have the luxury of taking for granted have been brought about by faculty. So what! There's always a generation gap. We always take for granted what others had to sweat for. That's just the way things are. Nostalgia is nice, but it's water under the bridge. It's not 1968—let's get on with business.

Not so fast. You see, there's a backwash to all this. It has to do with whether or not your college is doing its job, whether or not it has a concern for the education you're getting. One thing is apparent from the students we talk with. They feel a general lack of meaning or, more often, "relevance," in their coursework. And they seem bored. According to what we hear, many faculty don't seem to care about making their lectures interesting or entertaining, and some of the time it seems like they're really talking down to you. And then, they give you these ridiculous tests that nobody can do because they include material that wasn't covered in class, or they give these ridiculous tests that everyone can do and put them on ridiculous curves. If you happen to run into a great teacher, it's unusual.

Sure, this could all be due to the primary agenda of many colleges—research. There's a lot of rhetoric about improving education around colleges, but there's very little being done about it. And to be blunt, there is little incentive for faculty to get involved. If faculty are good researchers or competent instructors they can ride on that regardless of most other considerations.

But there is another side to this story. A big part of the problem has to do with students. Many of you act as if you're at college to be "given" an education.

For some reason many of you have it in your heads that you come to college to have things spelled out in class. You think your academic work is class assignments, class texts, and problem sets. If you're lucky you work your schedules so you and your buddies can share class notes. That way you can regularly cut class, which in a practical sense reduces your academic behavior to responding to the lectures. Papers are a chore because they involve original thought and creative synthesis. There's no excuse for a badly executed job. You may even have to use the library and pull all-nighters to get them done on time. If your teachers aren't entertaining, if they don't fill your heads with ideas while getting laughs at appropriate moments, the class is a waste and something to be suffered through.

Many of you really don't bring much into class. Maybe you got the reading or the assignments done. But you don't seem to grasp that there are things going on around you that relate to your class work. Many of you don't read newspapers, listen to news, or get a standard news magazine like *Newsweek*. You simply don't know what's going on in the real world you're heading for. We aren't necessarily talking politics here, but it's depressing when one mentions the Middle East and finds out that some of you think it refers to Ohio. You don't seem to care enough to know.

51

Some people might say that this is just the general apathy that characterizes your generation of students. But not us! We don't think you're apathetic—we think you're boring. And by choice, no less. You show little curiosity. And you see no reason to make any more effort to learn than it takes to gain your functional competence and check off the boxes that get you a degree. You don't seem to like to think hard, deeply, or often. "Intellectual" is not the thing most of you want to be called. Let's face it—that's not "fun stuff" to do.

Education is a two-way street, and it demands an active and interactive involvement, both by the faculty and by you. You can't sit there, think that learning is getting enough information from classes to do well on tests, and call that education. If this is what you call education, you're wasting your time and money, along with the faculty's time, energy, and expertise.

Remember, faculty are as bored by you as you are by them. They don't look forward to preparing for class when they sense that few are interested in the material, that perhaps half the class hasn't done the daily work, that too many haven't even bothered to show for class. It's next to impossible to draw creative connections and make metaphorical jumps with the material because the students will be lost.

If you're bored because your teachers are tedious and seemingly mechanical and your courses seem like exercises in "mandatory blandness," think about who takes those courses.

CHAPTER 5

SOME BASIC JOB SEARCH STRATEGIES

Many of today's college students are concerned about landing a job. These self-described "realists" are extremely anxious, and who can challenge their anxieties? The motivations that drive them, or even influence them, are founded on clear messages: "The job market is tight; good jobs are hard to find." "Money can buy you happiness." "This education is a costly investment; it should pay off." "College education is a means to an end, not an end unto itself." Whether these messages are true is not at issue; these messages hit their marks quite effectively.

VOCATIONALISM AND A LIBERAL EDUCATION

Proponents of liberal education cannot ignore "vocationalist" students whose values and educational decisions are pragmatic and utilitarian. The basic qualities of depth and breadth that outline liberal education, combined with the pursuit of personal, intellectual growth are features that should be included, not excluded, in the vocationalist's experiences. Jacob Neusner (1984) discussed one view of this dichotomy.

> A liberal education teaches students how to work, but it does not give them skills for a particular job. It teaches them the disciplines of logical thinking, clear and accurate expression, sustained analysis, but it does not give an easy formula for solving a specific problem. Whether students study chemistry, geology, sociology, or philosophy, whether they master a foreign language or mathematics, or history or religious studies, they learn nothing they can sell to an employer tomorrow, but they gain a great many things they can draw upon through a long career of useful work. (p. 90)

Neusner may be mistaken, however, about what liberally educated students can "sell" employers. Lynne Cheney (1986), chairperson of the

National Endowment for the Humanities, makes the case that liberal arts training is valuable in American corporations. Informal discussions with corporate executives suggest that broadly educated students are attractive prospective employees. Companies will offer specific training, but basic skills in critical thinking and communication form the groundwork for career growth and development. This has been borne out in studies by university career placement directors (e.g., Bechtel, 1984).

Students can combine the philosophy of becoming liberally educated with the pragmatics of marketability. Advice givers can give students a reason to challenge the myth that good job placement is a function of completing a list of "business skills" and replace this myth with a strategy for utilizing creative course selection. Here, the underlying rationale of chapter 3, "The Myth of the Academic Major," is put into a career planning framework. Chapter 5 emphasizes that a campus can become a good place to develop marketable skills, integrate coursework with experience, research personal life goals, and learn from business practitioners.

CAREER GUIDANCE

Career counseling and placement offices are the obvious campus resources for students' career concerns. In general, the career guidance process has several aspects:

- identification of skills, values, areas of interest, and personal traits;
- identification of careers that match these skills;
- exploration of these careers;
- preparation for these careers; and
- placement or interviews.

Career guidance specialists utilize a number of tools to accomplish the earlier tasks. Skill and interest inventories, computerized career planners with names like SIGI and Discovery (see Heppner & Johnson, 1985), and one-on-one guidance are basic. But these specialists' ability to combine academic experiences into this process is often weak if they do not know about or have access to the academic realms of their campuses.

Placement services, the last step in this process, have varied successes. Although engineers and accountants do tend to find jobs through campus interviews, too many students put their employment "eggs" into a single placement basket. They hope to get good corporate campus interviews during their senior years. They are bound to be disappointed. Most students do not get jobs through this route. This is not surprising because, as most career counselors acknowledge, the vast majority of positions available to students will not be represented by interviewers on campus.

Well-prepared students will have created other routes in their search process.

THE ROLE OF THE ADVICE GIVER

Students are encouraged to depend on career counseling offices. Only 32% of students surveyed in a recent Carnegie Survey of Undergraduate Studies reported that they received adequate advice on vocational matters (Jacobson, 1986). For many students, academic advisers are not prepared to discuss career-related issues in the academic advising process. Students who see college as a preparation for the job market have a hard time accepting that the conceptual skills they are told they are developing—analysis, logic, communication—are applicable. And most faculty have no clear picture of the nature of job markets.

Some points need to be stressed:

1. Career development is a process in which all academic professionals can participate;
2. Helping students ask the right questions is a crucial part of the process;
3. Students should be wary of those who tell them what to do; the student's personal situation is so central that the process must teach students how to find self-determined directions;
4. Most older adults can help students look at this process in a helpful, logical way;
5. Helping students look at the world of work with a critical and questioning eye is important.

Nonspecialists will certainly have difficulty working with some career issues, such as identifying skills, values, and potential areas of interest. On these issues, most advice givers rely on career professionals. It is important, then, for advice givers to be well versed in what their campus's career offices do and do not offer and to be familiar with basic career planning tools. Even if a referral is appropriate, advice givers retain their credibility if they can initiate some basic exploration processes with students.

Even the student who "has absolutely no idea what I want to do," or for whom "everything is so interesting I really can't decide" can be stimulated to go beyond these statements into more satisfying areas of self-inquiry. Delineating what students do not want to do helps them being to realize that what seem to be limitless decisions can be brought down to manageable terms.

Playing games like "close your eyes and visualize your perfect work day, from waking to bed time—tell me about it" can begin the exploration process. Questions revolving around life style, "Where are you living?" "Do you commute?" "What do you wear to work?" "Do you work inside or outside, alone or with people?" can help explore important variables, such as skills and values. Students can then begin to see how to work on their issues.

This kind of search process uncovers questions that students must answer for themselves. Equally important for advice givers is to begin to challenge students' assumptions about work. Many students do not seem to generalize the worlds they know into their views of working. It is hard for them to realize, for instance, that ski corporations and the "rock world" carry career possibilities just as do banks, accountancy firms, and the "high-tech" industry. Besides demythicizing their perceptions, students begin to engage the search process, formulate their own questions, and make up their own minds.

THE ACADEMIC COMPONENT

Faculty can play an integrating role by putting concepts and experiences into a unified package. Independent study, combined with work experience/internships, can enable students to monitor what they are gaining in the work place, take these experiences beyond the daily tasks of work, and give them the ability to reflect on their personal opinions with an objective outsider. Internships are a useful way for students to explore work options, gain skills, establish contacts, test perceptions against reality, learn about the hidden job market, talk with professionals in a relaxed setting, and have an opportunity to reject, as well as accept, possible avenues. And they may explore without the type of commitment that tends to immobilize many students who are in the process of exploring the job market.

The standard format for internships is a prearrangement between a school and a work place. In many instances, the work experience has an obvious tie-in to a curriculum (e.g., journalism students working at a newspaper), or it is an overt attempt to encourage students to explore the nonacademic world (e.g., Antioch College's semester of work/semester of school cycle). "Internship," as defined here, is a useful catchword for combining a work experience with an academically credited independent study agreement.

Any negotiated work experience that falls within an agreed set of parameters can be an internship. The ideal of an internship is usually to learn the skills and ways of the work place from a particular point of view and from an employment level at which the student is not yet thought to be ready to work. Consequently, internships must incorporate strong components of supervision, creativity, and freedom to learn. Supervision and mentorship are musts. When these parameters are met and the learning experience is truly occurring, pay is not always a vital factor.

Academic components can play a role in internships in three key ways:

1. Attaching academic credit to internships through independent study arrangements gives the internships some dimensions of credibility that can be very helpful to the student. Sponsoring employers frequently like the implicit attachments to the college that these relationships bring, and they also like the fact that a faculty member is paying attention to the student's involvement. It reduces sponsors' perceptions of the amount of responsibility they are taking upon themselves, and they like being partners in this venture.

2. The credit component also gives students a good opportunity to incorporate academic viewpoints into their experiences. Students can, for instance, do an academic study of the field they are interning in so that their own understanding of what is happening in their work situations is viewed from several perspectives. Take, for example, an internship in the emergency room of a hospital. The independent study component could include research on health care delivery systems specific to the population that uses that particular hospital, a study of how constant stress affects medical professionals, or a greater understanding of the physiological basis of medical trauma.

3. The faculty sponsors of internships can also serve as objective observers and sounding boards for students, helping them to assess the impact of their internships on their career directions. Students also can begin to get a sense of whether there really is a connection between a liberal education and its applicability in the work place.

STUDENTS' NETWORKS

Another facet of students' job research is learning to "network." Establishing networks is important to most people's social and professional lives. Although students can readily envision how internships and informational interviews have the potential to lay the groundwork for networking into the job market, they frequently do not make use of the networks they already have. Often they do not recognize these networks, or they have a difficult time using them.

Most students know people who can help but frequently do not recognize these people's ability to do so. Family members are often not perceived outside family roles. Even parents and friends' parents may be overlooked as good information sources.

The information network that students construct can be substantial. Internships and jobs may grow from networked relationships, but students' abilities to find appropriate people who can answer questions that published surveys and job category descriptions do not is what is really important. Questions like "If I were to walk into your office looking for a job, what would you like my background to be?" "What are your most and least favorite things about your job?" "What are your personal concerns abut free time with family?" "If you had it to do over again . . .?" People know the answers to these questions, and people like to talk about themselves.

This process can put students into an active mode and can encourage them to take personal responsibility for the directions they choose to take. Learning successful routes into the job market can be readily facilitated by the somewhat leisurely and noncommittal pathways that only students can take. The stakes, at this stage of students' careers, are low. Chances can be taken without much risk; failure is not punished with the cold realities of unemployment. On the other hand, the excitement of exploration can bring many unforeseen rewards including a solid basis for further searches and skill development.

ESSAYS ON THE JOB SEARCH

The essays in this section address issues of how students can combine the academic and extracurricular aspects of college into a coherent job exploration and life-goals planning strategy. The first three essays discuss "reality testing"— how students can match their perceptions of themselves and their aspirations against the realities of the job market. These essays also suggest ways for students to incorporate internships and academic coursework into these testing processes. The fourth essay provides examples of several students who utilized these strategies to construct fields of study that resulted in personally meaningful jobs. The final essay provides support for students who want to use college for the intrinsic joy of the learning experience without regard for vocational considerations.

These essays provide practical routes for action that students can readily take. The information can be translated into advice giving, into programs on college and the search for jobs, and into student handouts.

You'll probably be in the dark about your job future until you answer these four questions:

1. What is the big picture—and what are the little ones—for the field you want to work in?
2. What field of study is the one that will really do the trick for you?
3. What should you be studying (not the same as question no. 2)?
4. Is it an education or training you're after, and what are the differences?

"Reality testing" is the way to answer these questions. You need to take the ideas you have about school, relate them to the world of work, and bounce them around the court to see if they hold true under stress. One method of doing this is to "get it from the horse's mouth!"

Career planning guide books, government blurbs, and newspaper articles can only take you so far. They are generalized to the entire population. You, however, are you. You have a subset of specifics that you have to put into perspective. You need to talk with people in the areas you feel you want to pursue in order to integrate college effectively with your life in the world outside the campus.

Many of you students will graduate without jobs in hand. You'll eventually land jobs, and probably good ones, but they won't be laid at your feet. And for those of you who think you're employable, the picture may not be too rosy, either. It's an eye-opener for you active-bodied people to find that the realities of public accounting mean sitting all day long. And for those of you scuba buffs who went into marine biology to follow the Mediterranean romance of Jacques Cousteau's mystical adventures, it's an eye-opener to find that the real action in marine biology is in the saltwater marshes and intertidal mudflats of North Carolina.

The same is true for those of you who have your sights on professional degrees. What many of you think business or law is about may be a far cry from the day-to-day tedium of negotiating and drawing up contracts. People in these professions will tell you that professional schools don't prepare you for the nose-to-the-grindstone realities. They will tell you to do more with your undergrad education than putting together a slick package to get into an MBA or law program.

The slick package you put together is a marketing scam. But putting together a good education for yourself is an entirely different issue. You may find, much to your surprise, that your most marketable skills are learning to think clearly and logically, being able to analyze information and synthesize solutions, and being able to use language. Even the need for computer literacy may be a myth if you're looking for a job in a small business. Consider this from *The Chronicle for Higher Education*:

> Small-business owners look for interest and enthusiasm in the people they hire, rather than computer literacy—even if those people will use a computer on the

job. "There is little indication that computer literacy is an important requirement for learning how to use computers productively in small business," says Henry M. Levin, a professor of education at Stanford University. "Rather, interest and enthusiasm, reading and comprehension skills, and reasoning skills seem far more important." If students do take computer courses, they should focus on small-business applications of computers to impress potential employers, he adds. Mr. Levin and Russell W. Rumberger, a senior research associate, reached their conclusions after surveying 2,800 members of the National Federation of Independent Business. ("Study Finds," 1986, p. 28)

That same newspaper cites a report called *Corporate Ph.D.: Making the Grade in Business.* "It is not the content, but the process, of graduate education which transfers to business." Humanities PhDs in business and industry don't use their humanities knowledge; they use the skills—analysis, synthesis, writing—that they developed in school (Watkins, 1986, pp. 23–25).

The pros out there may tell you that a college education doesn't really train you for the real world. If you want to prepare for the real world, part of the responsibility for that preparation rests on you. For starters, you'll need a lot more information than you probably have.

Don't be afraid to call lawyers, chief executive officers, directors of research, assistant deans of graduate admissions, and the like. For the most part you are going to find that many of these people are flattered to be asked for advice. They're usually more than willing to tell you how they stumbled into their particular career paths, where they see the trends going, and what they deem valuable in your training and in your education. If you ask these people for this kind of information, not for jobs or personal favors, you'll probably get it because they have it to give. People usually take great delight in talking about something they know. In this case, it's their businesses and their lives. What could be easier for them?

Let's bring this strategy closer to home: Pose the same types of questions to your parents, older siblings, Uncle Vanya, and Auntie Mame. You may not appreciate the resources these people can be. Like you, your parents, older siblings, and relatives had successes and failures, doubts and frustrations. They can give you an intimate view of the day-to-day world, the things they have to put up with, and the rules of the game that are never spelled out in the courses you take. Equally important, your parents can give you a pretty good idea of the compromises they had (and still have) to make and the pressures their careers (or lack of careers) have imposed on their personal lives.

What you're likely to uncover from these discussions is information about the hidden job market, that nebulous area where 80% of all job openings exist. This area doesn't necessarily advertise, recruit, or even interview candidates; it has no special formula because so much action and flux exist. It's an area where "personnel officer," "application," "recruiter," and even "resume" may have no relevance.

Another insight contradicts popular college job hunt mythologies: Many new jobs on the current market are not with big corporations. Small businesses, say 100 people or less, may be where the action is. And it could be the case that entry level people in small businesses are given more independence, creative ability, responsibility, and latitude.

These are some of the critical issues you need to think about as you piece together your education. The whole point is that you don't want to flop around like a fish out of water. You want to look at college as a learning resource. You don't want to shortchange yourself. If using your education as a tool to enter the job market is your aim, it's your responsibility to put the parts together because no one else can do it for you.

Get a degree, get out, get a job. Is that your college cheer? If so, then the issue to confront now is whether or not your job stereotype has any match in reality. Most undergrads make synonyms of "business," "corporation," and "job" without having much of an idea of what goes on in corporations, what differences exist between corporations, or if life outside of corporations even exists. The same is true for your ideas about professions. Too many of you have no sense of the day-to-day world of a doctor or lawyer, whether these carry the glamour you have been led to believe, or have their own particular kind of tedium. And the "hidden job market?" Well, if you had any sense of it at all it wouldn't be hidden.

Christmas and Spring break times—when you let it all hang out, party, relax, visit with the relatives, pick up some extra cash—can also be just the right times to do some research. These breaks usually fall into the semester cycles at times when decisions for coming semesters are being made, and this research may also dovetail into summer jobs. It could be fun, and it will be work. But if you have some inkling that school should work for you, the converse is also true—you should work for school. At worst you may clarify what you're doing with school and your career plans.

One buzz phrase is pertinent here: the informational interview. What's important at this stage is to "get it from the horse's mouth!" We've said this before. Here's the strategy.

Don't assume you have a handle on any job market, even if you're in one of the "marketable" majors. Whether you're a PhD candidate in the humanities or an undergrad in electrical engineering, you ought to talk to the people who might be hiring you—not personnel directors, but CEOs, VPs, directors of divisions or labs, or the people who are actually doing what you think you want to do. Let your imagination go on this. You don't have anything to lose, and you can't really afford not to take this step.

Remember, anyone who has a job represents the fact that a job of that sort exists. Remember, too, that jobs are created. Trends and needs are as important as the status quo, and, especially in the small firms that have flexibility, the right person can stimulate the creation of a new job. It may not be so crazy to think about the front office of the Chicago Cubs as a place to work. You don't know if these options exist unless you make the effort to find out. But you won't make that effort until you believe that there's more out there than meets your eye.

Call to make appointments to talk with people—in any area you feel you're interested in, no matter how crazy you think it is. First you'll get a switchboard; ask for the name of the person in charge of the area you're interested in. Then you may get a secretary. At this point, you may balk! "Why would anyone in a senior position want to talk to me?" Because you are a student and that makes you interesting. Try this line on secretaries: "I want to make an appointment with

_____ . I'm a _____ College student in ABC and I'm doing some research." You'll be surprised how often this approach works.

Don't limit yourself to one or two places. Make as many appointments as you can. For your first few appointments schedule places you're least interested in. The first time you walk into an office you're going to feel like an idiot until you realize that the person you're talking to is a person too. This strategy will give you time to practice for the places you're most interested in.

Have a brief resume and your academic program outlined on paper. But remember, you're not going to be interviewed; you're going in to interview and, you hope, to hire an employer. Look like you mean business. Showing people your paperwork is helpful to them. You're asking for their opinions. They need information about you in order to personalize their advice.

You should be prepared to take the interview where you want it to go. Keep in mind you're talking to these people for their advice. You should have done a little research of your own by this point, so you can ask substantive questions. You don't walk into a development manager's office and simply say "What do development managers do?" Five pages of reading at the career center can brief you on this. You want to know more than a book's stereotype. What can this person tell you that books cannot? You want to know their views on what's going on, what they see as the trends, what they see as future career paths, and what they look for in a prospective candidate's background. But, most important, you want to get these people personally involved with you. You want to lay your program on their desks and get them to advise you on what they feel its strengths and weaknesses are and where you can beef it up to make you more substantive as a job candidate.

You will be surprised how flattered these people will be when you ask them for this kind of advice. Few students ever go to such people to find out their views on how students should look at their academic programs. For the most part, these people will show genuine interest in helping you out.

Now, at some stage of this process you're going to get into a bind. You're going to want to ask for a summer job or an internship. (Digression: A "job" is where you work at your current level of expertise where you generate goods or services for the business, and they pay you. An internship is a growth and learning experience under mentorship. It may have job qualities, but it's different.) That's a violation of trust. You set up this interview for information. You can, however, talk about "getting experience via internships" and where you can get them, or where they can refer you. When you bring up the issue, they'll know if they want to make an offer. And keep this in mind: Where before there were only "good ole boys' networks," nowadays there are "good ole girls' networks," too.

Now you're ready to go for the internship. Here's a hint—go to places where no formal internships exist. In many instances, these are places where no one has thought to create one. When you raise the possibility of creating one, you'll find yourself in a position where the only competition you have is your own ability to sell somebody on you.

64

What you've been doing at college may not make sense after you've researched the job market. You may have found that your coursework or maybe your entire school experience has no relevance.

Now is the time to reassess your options, especially if you've turned up some new possibilities from snooping around the world of work. Maybe you found positions, such as media expert in a social welfare agency, or special events manager for your local TV station, that don't require specialized degrees as much as proof that you can do the job. You also may have learned that these jobs will never hit your college's placement service, let alone the local newspaper. You've learned, in other words, that what's important is not so much the name of your degree but what you can actually do and how you pursue possible job options. Now's the time to be researching the campus components that will give you a strong and flexible field of study in order to access those options.

Track down the appropriate faculty and talk with them about what you've unearthed. Find out from them how your needs translate into coursework, even if you have to create the courses. If you're interested in trend marketing, print media, or hospital/community development, don't bank on mainstream marketing, journalism, or health education courses to focus on your concerns, but talk to faculty who teach these courses. Lay out your interests, and work with them to create special-topics courses or independent study. Faculty are your resources; their courses are not the only way to pick their brains.

If you're on a small campus, your task of finding the right faculty and setting up special arrangements should be pretty easy. On a larger campus, you may need some help. Once you have a direction, there's more to be done. Advisers, department heads, and deans may be necessary to help you cut through red tape. Many of the things you want to do may involve courses that seem inaccessible because they are designated "for majors only" or are offered at the graduate level. Also, many departments don't have obvious routes to sponsor internships for credit. But if your ideas and reasons are academically sound, administrators can help you figure the angles for getting access to courses and getting credit for internships. In many cases, tricks exist for cutting through the mire. On many university campuses, for instance, if you take a graduate course and can't get credit directly, the instructor may be able to give you independent study credit at a lower level. If internship courses don't exist, use independent study with a faculty member who will sponsor it.

Your departmental adviser should also have a good handle on how to use your minor and elective credits in creative ways. Some schools have quite a bit of flexibility built into their degree programs. English majors, for instance, often can incorporate such diverse elements as premed, finance, editing, publishing, and the literary market into their degree programs.

Finally, read your campus and local phone books. That's right! Your phone book contains a wealth of information if you know how to interpret it. There's more to a college than courses, departments, and student affairs. And there's more to the local town than bars and movies. Much of what goes on in the big city goes on, in one form or another, at a college or in a college town. Take advantage of that. College is a business. A glance through the directory should spark ideas: "administration," "business office," "athletic association," "legal counsel," "personnel," "public relations," "health center," "media division and news bureau," "planning office," "museum." The people who work in these divisions are professionals. They usually need help, and they are tuned into the campus. Students are part of their lives. And if it's not happening on campus, campus towns are also tuned in to students: city management, judicial affairs, risk management, parks and recreation. Just "let your fingers do the walking" and then follow the path.

An example or two are in order to give you an idea of a direction to take: Writing is the currency of academics. Faculty produce books, papers, and newsletters, ad infinitum. This hidden campus activity can lead you into an experience of the world of publishing and editing.

Whoever is producing these works probably can use some help. Professional journals, for instance, have editors who come from the ranks of professors. If someone on your campus is a journal editor, ask if you may help. There are few other ways to get experience in this area. Courses are few, if they exist at all, and job announcements say "experience necessary." Here's your path, between the cracks of this Catch 22.

New businesses starting up in town are good bets for the internship trail. When a local convention center began operations, a sophomore we know was asked to step in, under the direct supervision of the boss, to set up three major conventions. In exchange for no pay, the boss promised important connections and a surefire route to a job, plus the experience.

Remember, we suggest on this round that you go for the experience and not the bucks. If you have to do this stuff for nothing, it's worth it as long as you're learning a lot, are not taking away someone's paid job, and aren't being ripped off. Keep this in mind: Most places around campus and in town don't have regular internships established. You'll have to use your energy, imagination, and ingenuity to set up some appointments and sell these people on you. It's a two-way street as far as this goes. Your quality work benefits them; their internships give you critical experience to put your learning on a practical plane, to put something on your resume, and to provide you with a good reference.

If you handle things right, you might set up a semester's (or longer) internship convenient to your schedule. And, if you talk with your department adviser, you might also be able to work out credit coursework to go along with the internship. But this isn't going to fall into your lap without some major efforts.

Can your bachelor's degree be meaningful, personally satisfying, educationally rewarding, and marketable? We believe that it can. You will find out if you see past college departments and into colleges' underlying interdisciplinary nature. You have to unify your interests into a relevant field of study, and you're going to have to remember this theme: Academic majors are mythical illusions that can mislead you. How can you put the pieces together? Here are a few students' stories.

Lou asked this question: "How can anyone pursue international business without understanding both international finance, accounting, economics, and political, historical, and cultural affairs?" Lou's answer to this was to pursue French/international banking. Lou combined coursework in international accounting, business administration, economics, and multinational business finance with French language, literature, and culture, European history, and Western European political science. But as a French major, Lou still felt uncertain about marketability. So Lou identified the Paris banks that had offices in hometown Chicago, wrote to their Chicago offices in French, and arranged interviews to talk with them about international banking from the perspective of French banking. Once in the door, Lou managed to secure an internship for the summer in Chicago and an internship in the Paris offices while studying abroad. It was a combination of cultural/historical studies, basic business fundamentals, and language fluency that proved attractive.

For a second example, physicians don't deal with inanimate objects; they deal with people. And people aren't simply biological hosts for disease. They are individuals within a complex sociocultural milieu. Because doctors often deal with diverse populations, the ways in which people differ from one another culturally and ethnically can be important considerations for healing. Crosscultural views of health and illness can be critical to effective treatment. Pat believed premedical studies should be approached in this way and so pursued a field of study in social perspectives in medical care/premed. The program blended studies in medical anthropology, the history of medicine, ethics and moral problems in medicine and biology, sociology of racial and cultural minorities, sociology of medicine and medical care, problems in health care delivery, the Spanish language, and a cultural perspective on Spanish-speaking people in the U.S. with premed science. Pat graduated within the 4-year span and was granted early admission to two medical schools as well as to a program in hospital administration.

Chris's interest was in early American history. Despite the question of "What can you do with a history degree?" Chris pursued a personal interest in the life styles and customs of early American colonists. Chris wanted to be able to reconstruct the ways the colonists lived. To do this Chris combined work in anthropology focusing on archaeological methods, studies in English and Celtic folklore, and history focusing on colonial beginnings and its intellectual and cultural environment. Chris supplemented this work in England and Ireland

67

studying Irish folklore, 15th- through 18th-century society, Irish language, and creative writing. But what could Chris do with this? It seems a bit "academic." But Chris found that there is a world out there in historical reconstruction and interpretation that is geared to provide people with a view of "living history." Chris began to look into internship and work possibilities through museums and through the re-creation of historical sites. Chris succeeded in hooking into an internship at Plymouth Plantation, a historical reproduction of the original Plymouth colony. Chris's uniquely developed field of study opened up the avenue of creating "living history."

Jan's field of study was speech communications with a special focus on organizational behavior, conflict mediation, and organizational climate. Jan's courses had titles like Freedom of Speech and Ethics of Speech Communication, Communication Problems in Public Information Management, Film as a Business, and Interpersonal Communication Processes. One of Jan's goals was to explore law school with the intent of entering the field of entertainment law. On Jan's campus, the Assembly Hall was a full-scale entertainment operation that booked the whole range of big-time acts—Kenny and Dolly to the Grateful Dead, the Ice Capades to The Lipizzaner Stallions, and the Royal Danish Ballet to the Royal Bagpipe Regiment, not to mention big-time sports. Jan's internship, under the joint supervision of a faculty/administrator and the director of the Assembly Hall, resulted in her producing a "Casebook of Defensive Strategies for Arena Managers." To write this casebook Jan used the law library to research cases on personal service contracts for entertainers, liability issues, the effect of the dram shop act on public drinking in entertainment facilities, drug liability, and the like. Before writing the casebook, Jan worked in all parts of the Assembly Hall operation—accounting, legal counsel, events management, and publicity—to get a feel for how this book would be useful. Jan is now attending law school at UCLA where entertainment law is a strong program.

Lee was a dancer. The difficulties of being able to dance professionally were made clear by the dance department, and Lee wasn't sure if that was the route that would lead to personal fulfillment. Lee was also ambivalent about the lifetime of uncertainty of always having to be looking for jobs or auditioning for companies. Lee also knew that a dancer's knees can only last so long. When a national touring company came through town, Lee arranged to spend the next summer helping the manager work the tour. Lee was good at business and was pretty well organized, but the job of being in the background just didn't generate the energy of being on stage. Lee is back dancing now.

Stevie had diverse interests in the arts and sciences and a career goal of becoming a doctor. Stevie took the chance to bring together some very intriguing studies by becoming a premed/oboe major. Among oboe players a controversy exists about the resonance quality of oboe reeds made from artificial instead of natural materials. Fashioning a natural reed is quite a chore, and consequently artificially made reeds are quite attractive for practical reasons. Stevie completed a senior thesis on the biological and physical structures of both types of reeds to see if the best characteristics of both could be blended. For Stevie, science illuminated art in an experimental and aesthetic context. These studies also proved attractive to medical schools. Stevie is now an MD.

These illustrations hardly touch what you can do on a campus. Students study Japanese language, cultures, and computers; anthropology of play and community development; dance kinesiology, art, and therapeutic recreation; and natural systems biological pest control. The ways to make an academic environment give you a meaningful education depend only on your imagination and effort. The common thread of these illustrations is that none of these students pursued a major—though they graduated through majors. Their focuses were on a problem or field of inquiry that interested them. They used the flexibility inherent in many academic programs to build fields of study where the pieces of their educations fit together coherently. Their marketability emerged because their studies were both broad-based and specific, and because their academic portraits, gained through the process of constructing unique and coherent degree programs, stood out in innumerable ways. Because of how they pursued their studies they learned how to see into the hidden market which, by its very nature, is never advertised through normal placement and advising offices.

What these students did was integrate the concepts of personal growth, intellectual development, personal responsibility for their educations, and the potential for lifelong learning into neat academic packages. Not only did they learn the disciplines and methodologies of the departmental majors they worked through, but they learned the value and methodology of integration, connection, and creation. That's getting something out of college education.

So far, we've been telling you that you're probably wasting your time at school if you don't try to make good use of your college's resources. We've been trying to get you to buy into this with a "carrot and the stick" approach—you can make your education meaningful and still be marketable.

Our point is that with a goal in mind you can readily orchestrate college resources into a personally satisfying education. We've been trying to get you to buy into this by taking what we care about—meaningful education—and tying it to something many of you seem to care about—getting a job. But career goals aren't the only way to orchestrate your education. And to be frank, for many of you it's probably not the way to go. You could be leading yourselves down a garden path.

You see, our hidden message is this: You never arrive at your education; you're constantly going after it. Given the astonishing rate at which technology and new information change the fabric of the work place and society, your undergrad years may not be able to prepare you to meet the challenges of a constantly changing world. If you spend your time in school specializing around a career goal, you could find yourself obsolete because you neglected one of college's central purposes—learning for the sake of learning.

There's a good case to be made for coming to school with nothing more in mind than checking out the possibilities and fostering your curiosity. There's a case to be made for an eclectic education. Simply put, eclectic education aims at a carefully chosen, broad sampling of college possibilities. The strategy is based on something different than a career strategy.

Cathy, for instance, developed a strategy that "there are no good courses; there are only good teachers." She looked for a department with a minimum of courses required for the major and a maximum flexibility in elective courses. Her idea was this: The content of a course is no more important than the learning process. All the different ways that teachers could excite her to learn became as important, if not more important, than course content. Quality teaching became her criterion for course selection, not how courses would provide her with specific skills or knowledge.

Cathy's field of study themes did develop, of course. She gravitated toward the humanities. But she also studied social science theory. She found that social sciences helped illuminate many of the things she studied in the humanities. Abnormal psychology gave her some insights into *Crime and Punishment*, cultural anthropology helped her to understand Appalachian folklore, and descriptive grammar gave her the grounding behind teaching methodology as well as a sense of what good writing is about.

Cathy was completely turned on to learning, and her teachers inspired her to include an optional senior thesis in her studies. She graduated, feeling not only that she knew something about a lot of things, but satisfied that she knew how to learn about anything. Her education gave her confidence that she easily conveyed to others. She got a job as an editor at a publishing house, worked for a few years, and then went on to graduate school with financial support.

But there are other ways to go about an eclectic education. Ira made the theme of "personal intellectual development and let's see what life is all about" his goals for college and for his life style. Again, his strategy was based on the confidence that all students can effectively deal with the future if they use college to learn how to learn.

Ira centered his activities as a writer for the college newspaper, eventually moving up to the position of editorial page editor. Here he learned what "being informed" is all about. He realized that his studies meant more than cramming information in order to pass tests. He learned how to think, pick up on currents behind events, consider how thoughts and events affect how he viewed the world, and see how nuances and subtleties of happenings around him could affect major events and his daily life. Ira spent a year in England and graduated as a history major with no particular job in mind, but he looked forward to winging it and putting together some good adventures along the way.

You see, what we are talking about is common learning, learning that lets you become intellectually and socially empowered. That's the real idea behind your college education—not to become credentialed, but to become educated. Sure, it's easier to do with the security blanket of a career goal in mind. But you can just as easily do it with nothing more in mind than the learning itself. And what about jobs? There are always jobs—and good ones—for those who can think well.

CHAPTER 6

SCHOOLING BEYOND THE BACHELOR'S DEGREE: FACT AND FICTION

Postgraduate study—schooling beyond the bachelor's degree—is usually quite different from undergraduate work. Undergraduates considering postgraduate study frequently have little understanding of what the differences are, or of the implications those differences may have for their choices among postgraduate programs. This lack of understanding can lead to passive strategies for applying to postgraduate schools and may result in serious mistakes in students' postgraduate school choices. To avoid such mistakes, students need to understand the nature of postgraduate study; their choices of programs and schools can then be active and informed.

Whereas the undergraduate school application process can be somewhat haphazard and still result in a good education, postgraduate choices are often less forgiving. Coursework for undergraduate majors usually emphasizes foundations of a subject area and thus tends to have something for everyone. Postgraduate programs, however, are based on the field-of-study approach and tend to promote specific philosophical directions or areas of expertise. The directions of these programs are determined by the academic bent of the faculty who emphasize particular facets of their disciplines along with various schools of thought and ways of inquiry. Psychology departments, for instance, may emphasize behavioral or humanistic or psychoanalytic approaches; economics programs may emphasize quantitative or social-political analyses and may have supply-side or Marxist leanings; life sciences divisions may emphasize molecular biology or ecology programs; law schools may emphasize corporate or public interest law. If undergraduate students do not properly research the philosophical directions of the programs they apply to, they can end up "mis-matched" in programs that are incompatible with their own educational interests and beliefs.

Students also need to consider whether they are looking for "generic" programs or whether they want to pursue specific program options. Some law schools, for example, have programs in educational law, entertainment law, and environmental law. They may also have joint degree programs where students can concurrently earn degrees in areas such as medicine, public administration, or public health. Prospective law students need to consider not only whether particular law schools place their graduates into good firms but also whether these schools have specialty areas of study that are relevant to their interests.

Graduate departments may also offer a variety of programs. Psychology departments may have programs in social, quantitative, developmental, experimental, community, biological, and clinical psychology. Even within the same department, programs may have different philosophies and directions. Because these differences can all be significant, it is critically important for prospective postgraduate students to research thoroughly the philosophical directions and program options in the schools they are considering so that they can find the programs and the schools that fit them best.

In considering postgraduate school options, students must also be aware of the important differences among various types of postgraduate studies. In general, postgraduate studies take one of three formats:

- academic (e.g., MA, MFA, PhD);
- professional (e.g., MD, JD, MBA); and
- certification (e.g., teaching, social work).

These three categories obviously overlap. One can get an academic degree in the study of medicine or education; a social worker (MSW) is a professional; and those practicing medicine must be certified. These categories can be used, however, as a framework for discussing the different expectations and demands implied by these program formats.

A major intent behind academic graduate programs, for instance, is to engage graduate students as "apprentices." Ideally, graduate students work closely with faculty to combine coursework, research, and teaching experiences that will enable them to master their disciplines as well as the philosophical directions of their programs. Through the process of doing their own original research under the guidance of research directors, graduate students frequently have the opportunity to construct their own individualized fields of study. This graduate school process is intended to develop "novice professionals" with distinct areas of specialization who, for years to come, will be known as products of their programs or as students of their research directors.

In professional and certification programs, specific training, not apprenticeship, is the implicit model, especially during the early years. Professional school faculty implicitly state "We know what it takes to be a member of this profession, therefore do as we say." Certification programs, many of which are prescribed by law, make comparable statements: "Standards exist, and you must have specific academic experiences (e.g., courses, practica, internships) to verify that you have met these standards." Professional and certification programs are usually designed to prepare their students for specific jobs. Curricula are usually prescribed, and few elective options exist. Homogeneity among students' programs, not individuality, is the norm. When considering the possibility of entering a professional or certification program, prospective students should be aware that they will encounter these kinds of limitations in their educational freedom.

Prospective students also need to understand how the role of graduate assistantships differs between academic graduate programs and professional and certification programs. Such an understanding may assist them in choosing among the various postgraduate programs that interest them. In many academic graduate programs, for instance, students gain an important component of their training and education by serving as teaching or research assistants. Some programs even require such experiences. Many graduate students find that such assistantships are not only educationally valuable but are also excellent ways to gain collegiality with faculty and to increase job marketability. Graduate assistantships are also a significant form of financial aid. Many graduate departments routinely provide financial support for graduate students in the form of assistantships that usually pay tuition, fees, and a small monthly salary. Many undergraduates, particularly those at colleges that do not have graduate programs, are not aware that these opportunities for financial aid are available and, that they are, in fact, standard admissions awards in some departments.

Financial support in the form of assistantships is not standard for students in professional and certification programs. Because many of these programs do not have undergraduate counterparts (e.g., law and medicine), teaching assistantships are often scarce and are usually not seen as essential components of students' educational programs. In fact, some professional and certification programs may perceive assistantships as impediments to students' progress toward their degrees. Because assistantships are an unconventional option for students in professional and certification programs, prospective students who need assistantships as a form of financial support need to search out programs that are supportive of this option. Students in these programs are sometimes successful in finding appointments as teaching assistants in the curricula of their undergraduate emphases. Law students, for example, with strong bachelor's backgrounds in English may be able to teach introductory freshman writing courses, and medical students may be able to teach introductory science courses.

Advice givers cannot be expected to have first-hand knowledge of all aspects of graduate study. But they can serve as good resource persons and information sources for helping students make informed decisions about postgraduate study. Advice givers can help students raise appropriate questions and can direct students to people and places where those questions can be answered. Advice givers can discuss with students how postgraduate study differs from undergraduate work, the hurdles students are likely to encounter, the important roles that faculty mentors and fellow postgraduate students can play, and the realities of postgraduate students' life styles. Advice givers can help students consider the likely day-to-day realities of their prospective fields—for example, the increasing corporate control of medicine, the endless lab work and paperwork of a field biologist, and the 100-hour work weeks of some hot shot new MBAs—and how these realities are likely to fit with students' educational interests, personal and professional goals, and work styles.

Advice givers can also help students consider how assistantships may fit in with their plans for postgraduate study. With costs of education so high, many undergraduates reject postgraduate study as an option because of a misperception that they cannot afford it. Letting students know early in their undergraduate careers about the possibility of graduate assistantships may open the door for them to aim for postgraduate study. When they are ready to apply to schools they will also be prepared to look for programs where assistantships fit in.

Finally, advice givers can present an idealized model of what postgraduate study should be like and can help students use that model as a framework for evaluating particular programs. The process for making decisions about postgraduate study is similar for academic, professional, and certification programs alike and runs parallel to the job search process described in chapter 5. The strategies encourage students to self-identify goals, strengths, and personal desires, to interview a variety of people, and to conduct extensive research into various programs and schools. With these strategies, undergraduates will develop both a picture of what post-graduate study can be and a methodology for personalizing their options so that they achieve the "best fit."

ESSAYS ON POSTGRADUATE STUDY

The essays in this section propose a thoughtful process for choosing and applying to postgraduate programs. These essays present an idealized picture of supportive graduate and professional school environments and encourage students to use this ideal as a model for evaluating their possible choices. The information in this section can readily be used as the subject matter of programs that address career and postgraduate opportunities.

Graduate school—what is it all about? Is it another 2 to 7 years of the same old stuff that undergraduate life is made of—or is something different going on?

In its ideal form, graduate school is a whole new ball game. As an undergraduate, you were a mind, body, and spirit to be molded into a clear-thinking, responsible, adult person. As a graduate student, you have entered into your academic apprenticeship. Have no doubts about it: The approach to learning is different, the interactions between peers and between students and professors are different, and the power relationships are different.

For many of you, going to college was an expected necessity; it wasn't an option. Grad school is. Furthermore, it is likely that the research that went into choosing your college was sketchy and done without the aid of expert advice givers. Many of your possibilities were probably okay. At the graduate level there's much less leeway to err. Expert advice is available, however, and you can become your best source of information.

Graduate school, in its purest form, is a pathway in your search for intellectual fulfillment and admission into the "community of scholars," the PhD. You may have other interests in mind, like certification (e.g., teachers), licensing (e.g., psychologists), or skill development (e.g., accountants), but we'll return to these later. For now, it's the golden path we'll be discussing.

Graduate school is seen by many as a series of hurdles to jump. Some people sweat these hurdles; some don't. The formal hurdles are things like "coursework," "comprehensive exams" (comps), "qualifying exams" (quals), thesis, "preliminary exams" (prelims), admission to candidacy, dissertation, and "defense" or "finals." Different programs attach various meanings and weights to each of these hurdles, but the sweat and anxiety of grad school is usually associated with clearing them. It's not that the competition is tougher—once you're in, for the most part, no one gets Ds or Fs. But a grad student usually does not have the option to mechanically go through the paces of fulfilling requirements. Thus the overall game plan should be different if you are really going to dig into the academic world.

The hurdles of your graduate program should all be clearly laid out in program catalogs and departmental information sheets. If the program outline is not clear, haul up Red Flag Number One. When it's not clear, trouble could loom around each curve. The rules could change on you, the contract could be altered, and faculty could wield capricious power trips on unsuspecting grads. But let's assume that you've done your investigating and found the formal parts of your prospective program to be clearly delineated. Is that it? Graduate school should be much more. Grad school can give you the opportunity to completely immerse yourself in a self-defined interest.

And for starters, your courses serve several diverse purposes. Required courses are meant to provide a foundation for all members of a graduate program. They are your basics. But in many cases, they may also be an excuse to bring you together with your fellow graduate students in order to give you common ground and to help you develop collegial bonds. Electives serve a similar function. Besides giving you academic breadth, they give you another set of "contacts," people with whom you can bounce around ideas from perspectives other than those of your discipline's mainstream.

In the larger picture, courses are, at best, outlines. Putting the scholarship behind the courses into a coherent picture and digging into the substance are the keys to putting meat onto the bones of your education. Somewhere in this process an intellectual scheme will begin to emerge. Ideas will make sense; they'll connect to each other, and you'll begin to see yourself as part of the interconnectedness. How you see yourself fitting into this intellectual scheme defines your identity within your field of study. The hard work pays off at last. A scholar is born.

Beyond formal courses, your real growth is likely to come from small, intimate seminars, informal study circles, and late night discussions. Here you, your peers, and your professors hammer at the critical questions in your field, probing for answers and generating more questions. You are likely to develop your research interests and thesis topics as a result of these interactions—this is the real action of graduate school. This is also the beginning of your "academic apprenticeship."

Your fellow apprentices can have a profound effect on you. They are your office and lab mates, the people you talk with about your teaching and research problems. They are the sounding boards for your ideas and papers and your support staff for jumping the hurdles. The relationships you develop with other grads help to create the character of your graduate studies and are where much of your real learning takes place. The classmates with whom you enter graduate school are your "pledge" class. When your ordeal is over, when you are actively engaging your subject matter as a teacher, researcher, or businessperson, your fellow graduates are your coast-to-coast consultants; the relationships need never end.

Your peers are only one of the ingredients of academic fulfillment. Faculty are an obvious second factor. In your courses you can begin to develop peer relationships with professors. In graduate-level seminars you get your first hints that you are contending with many of the same intellectual problems that your faculty are. And you can begin to identify those faculty who will become your mentors—the people who will nurture your intellectual growth and buffer you from departmental politics.

This mentorship is a critical part of your apprenticeship. Your faculty mentors take you under their wings, help you formulate the questions you want to ask, and guide you through your studies into the first steps of your research. They are the people who serve on the committees that evaluate whether you have adequately cleared your hurdles. They are the people who help you "in progress" while you complete your research projects. The relationships you form with faculty should be much more than an occasional meeting with a faculty adviser to monitor your course schedules or your progress through a thesis. They should be consistent and invigorating.

Embedded in these student/mentor relationships are pathways to future opportunities. Your faculty mentors should be taking a personal interest in your intellectual growth as a part of a lifelong process. After all, your academic achievements reflect on them as well as on you. The quality of their program, their teaching and research agendas, and their concerns for the academic well-being of their fields are reflected in their graduate students. Lineages are commonplace in the academic world. For many years to come, you will be known as a product of such and such a program at the University of What's It State, or as "Dr. Who's student." The pride that faculty have in their programs and the personal ego factors involved with this identification cannot be ignored.

Your mentors are acutely aware of this identification, and they recognize the importance it can have on your career. They know that they should be guiding you into journal publications and conference paper presentations; that they should be helping you plug into research grants and fellowships; and that they should be introducing you to the prepublication network where the real collaborative work among scholars takes place. These scholars are the "consultants" from the previous "pledge classes" who have retained contact and expanded their own networks. They are the peers who pass judgment on one another in reviewing for various journals; they are the members of review boards that award research grants; and they are the departmental committee members who hire new faculty and make tenure decisions.

These are only some of the essential ingredients that are never mentioned in graduate program catalogs. They are, however, keys to rewarding graduate educations.

Don't assume that finding the graduate school best suited for you is a matter of making good grades, getting good test scores, and applying to a big name school. You may have been haphazard when you applied for your undergrad school. Maybe only one school really filled the bill, or State U was the only affordable option. But graduate school is another matter, and the guidelines for applying are different.

Most graduate and professional departments are looking for a "profile," a mystical combination of credentials that gives them good reason to believe you will be successful in their programs. They consider a host of evidence, some of which will surely include GPA. But there are grades and there are grades. The GPA you compute may not match their computation. Some schools are interested in your last 60 hours, and some may give more weight to grades in specific course types (e.g., science, math, or humanities). Some look for good grades during hard semesters.

Many schools are beginning to question the usefulness of standardized tests (e.g., GRE, LSAT, MCAT) as measures of potential to succeed. If they do request test scores, how they weigh them is often unclear.

Other criteria can also be critical. Letters of recommendation can make or break an application. Unless you've done more than simply serve your time in class, your professors won't have anything substantive to say about you. If your letter writers are alums or know members of your prospective program, all the better. The telephone, too, is a great 20th-century invention. If your letter writers care enough to follow through with a phone call, wondrous results are possible.

Although grad and professional schools are judging your credentials for that profile that predicts "success," they never quite spell out what that success is in objective terms. They know what they think, but their criteria may or may not jibe with your idea of a graduate education. Sure, medical schools want to produce skillful, thoughtful, caring, and self-sacrificing medical practitioners. They also want their students to score high on the boards and get dynamite residencies. And they look for credentials that predict this. Law schools, likewise. They want you to perform well in their curricula, pass the bar, make big bucks, and be a contributing alum. Most grad schools want to produce scholars, and it's their brand of scholarship they push. Is it lots of journal articles, masterpiece works of art in reputed galleries, or financial recognition by granting agencies?

Proof of your ability to succeed at graduate work can carry considerable weight regardless of your GPA. This means active participation in your field in terms of research, senior thesis, or work with faculty on projects. And these experiences are not just "resume items." They're a testing ground. How do you know whether you'll like it until you've tried it? Your undergraduate years are your best testing ground. The commitment isn't earth-shattering, but the payoff can be.

So you're ready for the search. That "prestige" grad department is the number one choice, right? Maybe not. For instance, you may never get to work with the big names who made the department so hot. Reputations lag, too. Those big names may be dead or gone elsewhere. And a school you might overlook because it lacks this "prestige factor" may have the faculty and programs best suited to your abilities and interests. And still other questions: What makes a particular program hot? How does it get this prestige and how, if at all, is this prestige passed on to you?

First of all, most rankings are dated by 5 to 10 years. Beware. How are rankings made? That's important to you. Some are merely the opinions of other experts. They're not based on specific criteria. Others are objective. How many papers by the faculty appear in big time scholarly journals? How many grads get good jobs or become whatever the department trained them to be? Some cite the existence of one or two research giants. Students who don't work for the giants may miss the boat.

Your inquiries can start with postcards to prospective departments. Request a graduate admissions package. Most packages include the department's own description of its admission criteria, faculty, and courses. You can get a pretty good idea of what credentials departments are looking for from this information. (In fact, if you get this package during your sophomore year, it may even help you plan out your field of study!) Some will have pretty hazy statements like "... an applicant's previous academic accomplishments, demonstrated potential for graduate and professional success, stated educational goals, three letters of recommendation from professors or supervisors, and these seven specific courses ...," which imply academic and experiential criteria. Or, "... applicants should pay special attention to the personal statement and should fully describe (a) research, teaching, or other career interests; and (b) past relevant experiences." What have you done that proves to us that we're the program for you, and vice versa? Some departments have strict point systems where you can figure out your chances before you even apply.

But don't be bowled over by their blurbs, how pretty their courses look in the catalogs, or the impressive list of faculty research interests. Colleges usually list far more courses than they actually offer, and course titles do not necessarily reflect current content. Shifts in faculty interests, departures, and retirements may leave a department with nobody to teach those courses. Or maybe they'll offer the courses by someone without the expertise to teach them. The faculty you're interested in working with may not be around for the next few years. Faculty are transient beings. They take off to do research elsewhere and take jobs at other schools on a regular basis. Some have quotas on the number of students they take, so even if they're around, they may be inaccessible. And some look great on paper but are so hard to get along with that they can't hold on to grad students. These examples are more frequent than many departments care to admit. You have to be careful if you make your plans around blurbs and catalogs.

Don't assume that good faculty are only at major schools. Budget problems, departments locked up by tenure, and fewer tenure track jobs at big schools have led many hot-shot young faculty to smaller schools. Schools that lack the prestige factor are frequently places where exciting things are going on.

Consider carefully the nature of the curricula at the schools you are considering. Each graduate program tends to teach its own "school of thought." If, for example, an economics department leans heavily toward mathematical modeling, it may be difficult to do social-historical research.

Whether it's law school, med school, an MBA program, or doctoral study, there are many ways to look into the options. Here are some tips.

Talk with your teaching assistants if you are on a university campus. If not, visit your friends at a university campus and talk to TAs there. They're graduate students and have recently gone through the grad school application game. They may know what different schools are doing and how to avoid some of the pitfalls. Also, many of these students are on top of the trends in their fields. They are good first sources of information.

Talk to your professors. They are plugged in nationally, and they are colleagues with the faculty at other colleges. Faculty are on top of current research. They attend national conferences, present papers, and sit on governance committees. Faculty can help you get a handle on how to apply to a school in order to work with certain other faculty. What should govern, in large part, the schools you consider are the people you will be working with, not the "name" of the school.

Check the journals in your field. Find out who's publishing in your areas of interest. These are some of the people you may want to work with. You'll be able to find out where they are because it's listed under their names in their articles. The publications these people write will give you the best sense of what they are up to. Likewise, keep an eye on the conferences in your field. Departments get flyers on these continually. If you can, attend. You'll learn what's going on and meet people who may be important to know. At the very least, write for the conference program to get the names of people who are presenting papers. You can always write to them for copies of their papers.

Once you have this information, write to individual faculty instead of a "generic" letter to the graduate school or department. You can mention that you've read their articles and that their ideas are interesting to you. Explain your background and your interests in coming to study with them. If they know you want to study with them, you could find yourself with a faculty mentor who can ease your way to admission, financial aid, and the outline of your graduate study.

Finally, visit the schools you're interested in or have been accepted to. *Don't choose a graduate school blindly*. By talking with grad students and faculty at these schools and by getting a look at the facilities, you can find out if what you expect from the place is, in fact, there. This could be your most crucial step, yet very few people take it. The real answers to your questions, and by this stage you should have plenty, are going to be given face-to-face. Ask students what they like and dislike about their programs, if they have regretted the choice and why, and what people are doing upon graduation. You've been accepted; you have nothing to lose and very much to gain at this stage. And remember—what you're looking for is a solid, supportive academic environment that is both professionally and personally satisfying.

Being a graduate student, especially in nonprofessional programs, is akin to a medical internship. The higher-ups know you have the stuff to do the job; that was a condition of your admission to the program. But there's lots more to learn. And they have you over a barrel. You need their expertise, and you need their credentials. The pay, when you get it, is lousy, and the hours are long. It doesn't sound all that attractive to the outsider. Why would anyone want to go through this process?

The "purists" are in search of intellectual fulfillment. They seek knowledge. They enjoy posing questions and finding answers. And the "pragmatists" want the credentials. The PhD, MA, EdD, PsyD, and MSW are necessary keys to otherwise locked doors. The credential goes hand-in-hand with the search for knowledge. You need the degree to gain formal entrance into the community of scholars.

All of these concepts are pretty ethereal, though, and don't give a good idea of what really goes on in a grad's life. How about money, housing, and a social life? Does life go on hold?

Many undergrads dismiss the prospect of grad school because they think it's unaffordable. This is not true in many cases. Colleges often pay you. Teaching is an essential ingredient of the graduate education process, and teaching assistantships are awarded as a form of financial aid. TAs usually get 50% appointments that can include tuition waivers and enough monthly stipend to get them by. Hold back on the caviar, accept cockroaches for a few more years, and you can make it pretty easily.

These teaching experiences are a great way to help you organize and discuss your academic interests. Any competent biologist can explain gene splicing to another biologist, but explaining its mechanism and relevance to a first-semester freshman taking a life science requirement is another matter. That's an academic art form, and, from a broader perspective, it plays an important social role. To explain your field to undergraduates helps to create an informed public, a public that decides on questions of support and policy. If you plan to be an academic, a vita with teaching experience will probably enhance your marketability.

Other forms of financial support? Some are obvious and some you need a shovel to find: Research assistants help out in labs and libraries. If you're lucky, an RA-ship is awarded to fund your own thesis research. Grads are the campus workhorses. They do academic advising and administration, and they find live-in jobs in residence halls as advisers and directors. Once in a while, a freebie comes along—that cherished fellowship—a no strings grant to do your own work.

Money may be tight, but it's available. One major caution. If you've been accepted to a program that normally has graduate funding and you don't get any, think twice. Funding is a form of commitment by the program to you. With funding, you've become their investment. If they don't think well enough of you to give you an assistantship, they may not want you for more than "filler," to keep their numbers up. And this will be reflected in how you're treated. It's a two-tiered system. Grad assistants are the "in group" apprentices. They get preferential treatment, office space, mailboxes, supplies, training, and attention. This is critical to graduate success. Go where the funds are waiting for you.

Now that you're a grad, you're in limbo. You're a long-term, broke transient. Your roots will be shallow. That beautiful ranch house or high-rise condo is on hold. Family housing, grad dorms, and student slums may be life-style necessities. Social life is different, too. Your department can be the center of many of your nonacademic activities. Softball team/potluck dinner combos create a great ambience with ready-made friends. It's all part of your new network.

These are nice daydreams about graduate school. They are what we all wish our graduate school experiences were like. But if you talk to those who have been through it—and that's your major research task—you may find that all this is illusion. Departments have politics, back-stabbing, rivalries, jealousies, and fights for space, money, and assignments. Grad school folklore abounds with stories about departments changing requirements on students in midstream, faculty being inaccessible or unprepared for class, professors unwilling either to advise or assist students in their professional development, and students whose relationships with their advisers deteriorate until leaving the program is the only option. We all know of grad students who can't find desk space in their own departments, are "exiled" because they don't buy into the "departmental line of thought," and are left to fend for themselves. It's not hard to find those who will tell you that graduate school can be a nasty, brutish business. And, frankly, sometimes it is.

But it doesn't have to be that way if you take the time to think about what you want out of grad school and find the school that will be best suited for you. The process is akin to the search for the perfect job. Hard work will pay off.

Postgraduate fields of studies have their shining stars, and nowadays the professions seem to be bright in the heavens. In particular, we're talking about law, medical, and business schools, but the story holds true for fields like clinical psychology, veterinary science, and journalism, too. The professional route has a different flavor than the graduate route and its own surrounding mythology.

Undergraduates frequently use generic academic labels. "Pre-law," "premed," "pre-journalism" and "business" designations are security blankets students use to display intentions. They have little bearing on admissions. Law school admissions are based on grades, LSAT scores, and mumbo jumbo. MBA admissions are based on grades, GMAT scores, and mumbo jumbo. Med school requires 1 year of biology, 2 years of chemistry, 1 year of physics, maybe calculus, grades, good MCAT scores, and mumbo jumbo. Now let's talk turkey: mumbo jumbo and strategy.

Most of what you hear about applying to these schools is general information that doesn't necessarily hold when you look at specific schools. Letters of recommendation, prior relevant extracurricular experiences, volunteer work, and membership in social, service, or honorary organizations may or may not play a role in admissions decisions. It's all school-specific, and schools never spell out the whole story in their application packets. In fact, some never spell it out, period. For instance, when a school tells you that their students' GPAs range from 3.3 to 4.0, what they are looking for, in the main, is diversity in the applicant pool and a large number of nonrefundable application fees. Even though the range is from 3.3 to 4.0, how many 3.3s are chosen from the great number who apply to the good schools?

College bookstores are loaded with guides to professional schools. Most professional organizations publish their own handbooks, too. Noteworthy are yearly additions of *Medical School Admission Requirements*, *Veterinary Medical School Admissions*, *The Official Guide to U.S. Law Schools*, and *The Official Guide to MBA Programs, Admissions, and Careers*. These books recite the "party line": facts, figures, and procedures. You can learn quite a bit from them. They usually list accredited schools in the U.S., admission requirements, a freshman class profile, and they may (e.g., medical school) list the in-state/out-of-state admissions ratios. These books are a necessary first step in the application process, but they're not definitive. You need more information and advice. And, ultimately, you can be your own best adviser.

To put together your own story in a way that will help you plan your undergrad courses and activities, you should read these handbooks and check out prospective schools a few years in advance. For the latter, postcards to admissions officers is all it takes. Admissions packages can give you an idea of what schools are looking for in an applicant's profile. Sometimes these packages are very specific, although one law school admissions officer we talked to doubted that many students read these packages. "Their personal statements didn't even give us a hint that they read our literature." These admissions officers can be your best source of specific information and guidelines, especially for the sort of stuff that doesn't ever appear in writing. You can readily locate them through your campus preprofessional adviser (your obvious primary information source), at the preprofessional conferences held on many campuses, through the wonders of Ma Bell (admissions officers are very willing to talk to you), or by visiting their campuses.

Forewarned is forearmed. If you babble generic questions, you'll get generic answers. When you talk to these people, be prepared. They have the answers to most of your questions and are usually very straightforward, albeit from their school's point of view. After all, they want you to apply to their schools in order to have a good admissions pool and to collect that nonrefundable application fee. They won't lie, cheat, steal, or deceive, but if you talk to representatives of four different schools, you'll get four different philosophies and strategies for becoming a professional in your chosen field. At this point, you're on your own. You are the "consumer" who's about to spend 2 to 6 more years, not to mention megabucks, investing in your future. Most students spend more time buying a new car than shopping for the right school.

Some of the things you read and hear might surprise you. At some schools "rigorous" coursework counts more than what major you've completed; good grades in hard courses during heavy-load semesters sometimes give you bonus points; certain types of courses are sometimes weighted (e.g., writing for law school; math for medicine and psychology); some schools never read your personal statement except to verify it with your standardized test writing sample; some schools don't bother to read letters of recommendation unless written by alums or professors; your undergraduate major does make a difference; your undergraduate major makes no difference at all; your extracurriculars do/don't carry weight, and especially with so much resume padding going on, without proof of substantial involvement in nonclassroom activities, who knows if you're making lists or really helping out in the community?

Now, stop. Think it over. Is the search process done now that you've checked out the school options? Not quite. You have to check out your inner self, too. Does the profession match the person, or are the rewards of the job—bucks and status—the attractors? Ask yourself why you want to pursue law, upper management, or doctoring. It isn't enough to say " I want to make a good living, and I want to work with people." You can do this by opening a bar. You like science, too? Put an aquarium in the bar. Nor is it enough to say the buzzword "business," or "I want to work for a corporation," unless you know the scope of businesses that attract you or have a sense of the diversity between and within corporations.

In the same way that you interviewed admissions officers, consider interviewing professionals. They're not cloistered in forbidden towers. Most everyone has a doctor and many of us even have one living next door or somewhere among our aunts, uncles, and cousins. Does your myth match their reality?

Take doctoring, for instance. In the old days, doctors rode into town, hung out their shingles, and became established entrepreneurs. They ran their own shows, hired some helpers, and made out pretty well. Nowadays, with the swing toward private, corporate control of medical service delivery, doctors are becoming wage earning employees with established working hours, union dues, and overtime pay. And those in private practice are finding themselves supporting, more often than not, their insurance companies.

Tomorrow, being a doctor won't conform to the stereotypes you now hold. With the current swing, the administration of health care delivery is becoming a hot "new" profession. If your buzzword is medicine, but the doctor part isn't necessary, there's a growing area of concern. Those entering the medical field will have to consider the problems of health care delivery to various populations, the role of government, the battle between the insurance agencies and the legal profession on medical competence, and health maintenance organizations. And, as the doctor market tightens because of hospital cutbacks, the independence factor of the old days will be gone. If you want to help people who have medical problems, there's more than one road to travel. Talk to the pros. They have the inside scoop.

Finally, you need to consider what you're doing with your undergrad program. Premeds who have no intention of being biologists should rethink why they are biology majors. There is nothing inherent in a biology major that will better prepare you for med school than other options. You could just as easily study health policy, science education, science journalism, philosophy, or cultural anthropology. *The Medical School Admissions Requirements 1985–86* (Association of American Medical Colleges, 1984) indicates that majors don't seem to play much of a role in the admissions game. Finding what your interests are and following up on them could help you build that "back-up" field in case your GPA points you in another direction. Or, if your career goals don't change, you will also end up having an educationally and personally rewarding complement to your medical education.

Law school runs a parallel course. The media report that a lawyer glut exists. Does this glut affect what you want to do with your law degree? Are some fields still wide open? Not everyone goes into litigation and courtroom law. Lawyers find jobs with government agencies, as general counsels for corporations, as bank estate planners, and in health law. Combining a custom-fit undergrad degree with a law degree may find you working wonders: engineering and patent law, family studies and divorce law, American studies and civil rights law, theater management and entertainment law. The list is as long as your imagination. Is it a useful strategy? It gives you at least three options: Use your undergraduate degree, use your law degree, use the combo. It gets you out of the generic political science/pre-law syndrome and gives you your own education.

Does corporate or big-firm law still haunt your dreams? Find a lawyer and get the score. To them time is big bucks, so you have to be professional about it. Most firms have a lawyer involved with recruitment. Write a letter. Request a short interview. Don't show up in your Levi 501s and expect much credibility. That's not their world.

"Business." What isn't business? You ought to consider whether an MBA program will get you what you want in the business world. For one thing, MBA programs are often redundant with undergrad business programs. For another thing, many students have developed "business" skills without even knowing it. Personnel and organizational management and computer programming are things many students learn in liberal arts programs. The management skills can be learned anytime; they're your tools.

On the other hand, what's business all about that makes it so attractive to you? Those lucrative entry level jobs that start at $50,000 in investment banking are often filled by "raccoons," new MBAs who have perpetual saggy-eye masks from 100-hour work weeks with no vacations and divorces hinging on every late night.

Don't be fooled by simply going after GPA, test scores, and glitz. Develop breadth of study with the ability to think critically, and present yourself coherently and with style. This is where the payoffs really are.

CHAPTER 7

A PRIMER ON COUNSELING SKILLS: IDENTIFYING, HELPING, AND REFERRING TROUBLED STUDENTS

A physics professor at a large Midwestern university wrote the following to the vice chancellor for student affairs.

> As a professor who sometimes teaches large service courses, I am often in the position of trying to respond to students with a variety of problems they want to share with some adult—even a physics professor. And yet, like most of my colleagues, I am not trained to deal with these. Beyond urging them to go to the Counseling Center, is there any advice to give? Any guidelines that would help us recognize the more serious problems?

This professor's concern is shared by many campus professionals. Despite high profiles and excellent services offered by college mental health services, students rarely turn first to professional counselors to talk about problems. Academic advisers, faculty, teaching assistants, and residence hall personnel, by virtue of the frequency and nature of their contacts with students and the respect students have for them, are often seen by students as more logical first contacts for advice and support. These campus professionals are often the first, and sometimes the only people, to recognize that students are not functioning well, academically or personally. Examples abound. Journalism students write about personal problems in their journals and papers for class. Premeds become upset when they fail to do well in required science classes. Academic advisers see students consistently dropping classes or not completing work. Teaching assistants see radical drops in students' performance over the course of a semester. Residence hall personnel see damage to property, alcohol abuse, and suicide threats.

What can advice givers do when they suspect a student may need help with a personal or academic problem? What is the appropriate role to take? How involved should advice givers be? What are the risks that advice givers may make the problem worse? How do advice givers know when they should be worried about a student? When appropriate, how should advice givers transfer the responsibility for helping students to the mental health professionals on campus? These questions will be addressed briefly in this chapter.

This chapter, unlike the preceding chapters, is written in the second person and is directed to YOU, the advice giver.

To begin, it is important to consider what the appropriate role of advice givers might be. Above all, it is important not to assume that a distressed student is being taken care of somewhere else. For a dramatic example, you should know that suicide is the second leading cause of death among college students and that many, if not most, of the students who make suicide attempts have not been under the care of a mental health professional. Does this mean that you are responsible for the lives of the students you come in contact with? Yes, in part. It is important to make sure that someone is taking care of the student in need. This means that you need to do more than show genuine interest. You need to be cognizant of distress signals and referral resources, and you need to know how to refer. The goal is to try to prevent problems from becoming serious. A little time and attention from you can be of critical importance to students.

WARNING SIGNALS

There will be times when something you observe about a student's behavior or manner will cause you to consider approaching the student. There are many signs that a student may be experiencing problems. We can begin by breaking these signs into categories.

Problems With Academics/Career/Major

1. dramatic decline in academic performance;
2. drop in class attendance;
3. pattern of dropping classes or asking for extensions;
4. severe procrastination or difficulty concentrating;
5. incapacitating test anxiety;
6. severe reactions to a poor test/paper grade;
7. lack of alternative goals when doing poorly;
8. overly high academic standards that aren't being met;

9. chronic indecisiveness with regard to major/career or dissatisfaction with major;
10. unrealistic career goals;
11. inadequate study skills, reading speed, or comprehension;
12. extreme fear of speaking or participating in class; and
13. doubts about ability to succeed in school.

Unusual Behavior

1. dependency: The student wants to be around you all the time or makes excessive appointments to see you;
2. lack of interest in prior activities, withdrawal from usual social interactions, seclusion, unwillingness to communicate;
3. significantly increased activity such as extreme restlessness, non-stop talking, inability to relax;
4. suspiciousness, feelings of being persecuted;
5. inappropriate or bizarre conversations such as talking nonsense or being unable to carry on a coherent conversation;
6. unusual irritability, outbursts of anger, unexplained crying, aggressiveness, excessive worrying or anxiety;
7. significant decline in personal hygiene, standards of dress, or grooming;
8. unusual acting out such as a change from normal socially appropriate behavior; being disruptive or aggressive; persistent lying or stealing;
9. signs of eating disorders: significant weight loss, binging/vomiting, secretive eating; and
10. alcohol or drug abuse or other self-destructive behavior such as cutting self or being accident-prone.

Signs of Depression

1. inability to concentrate, impaired memory, indecisiveness, confusion;
2. changes in appetite such as complete loss of appetite or compulsive eating;
3. inability to find pleasure in anything or dissatisfaction with life in general;
4. exaggerated guilt or self-blame for present or past events;
5. exaggerated feelings of helplessness and hopelessness with regard to the present and future;
6. loss of warm feelings toward family or friends or loss of self-esteem;

7. crying spells or marked lack of response to normally upsetting events;
8. sleeping difficulties including insomnia, early wakefulness, or excessive sleeping;
9. unexplained headaches, digestive problems, anxiety or panic attacks, or other physical symptoms;
10. chronic fatigue and lack of energy; and
11. neglect of responsibilities and appearance.

References to Suicide

1. feelings of helplessness, hopelessness, worthlessness;
2. preoccupation with death; giving away valued possessions; and
3. thoughts or threats of suicide or plans for suicide. *All references to suicide, whether directly or indirectly stated, should be taken seriously and referred to a campus mental health professional. Immediate referral is indicated when the reference to suicide or your subsequent discussion with a student about suicide indicates any plans or previous suicide attempts.* A more complete discussion of suicide prevention strategies is found in the essay that follows entitled "Why Do People Kill Themselves: Suicide and Suicide Prevention."

Life-Circumstance Concerns

1. death or serious illness of a family member or close friend;
2. illness (loss of health);
3. problems in dating or marital relationship, problems with roommates or family members, parents' divorce;
4. extreme shyness, lack of social skills, difficulty in making and keeping friends; and
5. severe homesickness, graduation anxiety.

Although these signs and symptoms may serve as warnings that a student is in distress, most of them do not necessarily mean that a student has a serious problem that warrants psychological help. (References to suicide, as noted earlier, are obvious exceptions.) In general, the more of these behaviors you observe, the more cause there is for concern, particularly if the behaviors persist over a period of time. These are signals that suggest that you should consider expressing your concern to the student.

WHAT TO DO: A "HOW TO" FOR ADVICE GIVERS

Your first step in expressing concern is to set aside a time and place to talk to the student where you know you will not be disturbed. You should approach the student as an interested, concerned human being rather than as an authority figure who knows what is best for the student. You might begin by describing the specific behaviors that have raised your concern.

> For example, "John, I've been becoming increasingly concerned about you for several weeks. Your performance on your papers has dropped significantly, you've stopped participating in class, and you generally look like things aren't going very well. I don't want to pry into your life, but I'm wondering if there's something worrying you that you might want to talk about." Or, "Sarah, I've noticed that you seem to have stopped going to class, are sleeping through meals, and your friends tell me that you have stopped talking to them and going out with them. They're very worried about you and frankly I am, too. I wonder if there's something bothering you or worrying you that's making you react in these ways. I don't want to pry, but I'd really like to try to help. Would you be willing to tell me what's causing these changes in you?"

It's important that you describe specifically to the student the behaviors that have raised your concern. You should avoid global statements like "You've been acting strange lately." Such statements give the student no real information and may lead him or her to feel judged, self-conscious, or defensive.

If, after describing the behaviors that concern you, the student does not seem willing to talk, you may want to (a) tell the student about the mental health resources available on campus and how to use them, or (b) contact one of the mental health professionals on campus and ask for advice about how to proceed. Either way, you should make it clear that you can be available if the student changes his or her mind and wants to talk at a later time. If the student does begin to talk to you, you need to keep the conversation going long enough to assess whether the student needs additional help. The steps described in the next sections outline a process to use in talking with the student, whether you or the student initiates the conversation.

WHEN THE STUDENT COMES TO YOU

When a student comes to you and says, in some way, "I've got a problem," what should you do? You need to keep four goals in mind:

1. Disclosure: You need to help the student describe his or her situation and feelings in enough detail that you can decide how to proceed.
2. Acknowledgment: You need to communicate respect and concern for the student and you need to make it clear that you have understood the information the student has shared.
3. Action: You need either to help the student decide what direction

to take or to help the student take a different perspective on a situation.

4. Referral: You need to know how much time and energy you're willing or able to spend in helping the student, and you need to know how to refer when you've reached your personal limit.

Disclosure

Most students, in bringing up a problem with you, will be confused, upset, or frightened. Under these circumstances they may not be as articulate as you might like. Suppose a student comes to you and says, "I want your help." You need more information before you will really know what the student needs. There are several key components in getting the student to disclose:

1. Ask open-ended questions or give open-ended directions. Open-ended questions usually begin with words such as what, when, who, where, how (e.g., "Tell me more about what's going on"). They elicit more than yes or no answers and encourage elaboration.
2. Communicate with encouraging nonverbal cues. Examples include a comfortable amount of eye contact for both you and the student, a relaxed, open, interested body posture, and a calm tone of voice.
3. Focus on the student's story rather than your own. If Chris tells you about a problem with test anxiety, don't jump in and say, "Well, I've had test anxiety too! I remember the time I ..." Your kind of test anxiety may have involved factors quite different than Chris's and may make Chris feel like the only one with this type of problem.

Acknowledgment

When talking with the student it is important to acknowledge what the student is facing. This acknowledgment should demonstrate your understanding of both the factual content of what is being said and the unique emotional impact of those facts on the student. For example, if a student starts crying when talking to you about a test grade, you might say something like "You seem to be feeling pretty upset. This kind of situation upsets different people for different reasons. What part of this situation is most upsetting for you?" By making it clear to the student that you are interested in his or her concern, by showing understanding, by communicating that these kinds of problems happen to normal people, and by conveying that individualized reactions are normal, you help the student feel less "freakish" for having the problem. This result, by itself, often makes the student feel better. Also, because the student will have felt your genuine concern, it will be easier for you to refer the student later, should it be necessary.

Active listening principles. Your responses in both "disclosure" and "acknowledgment" situations should involve active listening principles, particularly "paraphrasing" and "reflection of feeling." Although many situations will involve both paraphrasing and reflection of feeling, these components will be described separately to illustrate them more clearly.

Paraphrasing is an attempt to check whether you have understood the content of what a student has said. Paraphrasing involves saying the information back to the student in your own words, without including your own values or ideas. It is often not as simple, however, as "parroting" what a student has said. Instead, you should summarize the essence of the conversation in simple, clear terms and in a supportive tone. For example, suppose a student says, "My roommate is driving me crazy! One day she's friendly and talkative and then she'll change and she won't say a word to me for days." A good paraphrase might be, "You really don't know what to expect from her—she isn't consistent." Paraphrasing has several important benefits:

1. It helps ensure eventual accuracy. You are trying to capture the essence of what is going on. If you play it back, the student can tell you if you are missing something important. For example, the student with test anxiety may be more concerned about pressure from parents than test performance per se. You need to hear the student out and avoid jumping to conclusions.

2. Paraphrasing may help the student reformulate the problem more precisely, accurately, simply, and logically. If the information does not make sense to you, you can admit your confusion and say, "I don't quite understand what happened after X." When your questions lead to a reformulation of the problem, the student can sometimes go on to solve the problem.

3. Paraphrasing, like head nods and "uh-huh's," often encourages the student to continue telling you the things you need to know without being unduly influenced about what to say.

4. It is comforting to the student that you are interested enough to try to get the information straight.

Many well-meaning people fear being judged as "stupid" or "unfeeling" if their paraphrasing is initially inaccurate. This is typically not the student's response. After all, if the student thought the issues were simple and easily understood the conversation would not be occurring in the first place. More typically the student will feel cared for and respected.

Whereas paraphrasing helps you make sure you have understood the facts of a situation, reflection of feeling conveys that you are empathizing, that is, understanding how and why the student might feel that way. For example, suppose a student says, "I guess I'll have to take the class over ... but I'll probably just flunk it again," an empathic response would be, "You're worried that you're not going to be able to pass this class." A nonempathic response would be something like, "Have you considered getting a tutor?" The former reflects the student's attitudes, feelings, and reactions, whereas the latter does not.

Along with verbal content, tone and quality of voice, rate of speech, facial expressions, and body postures all provide clues to what the student is feeling. Although it will not be helpful if your feelings are as intense as the student's, empathy is genuine only if you experience some fraction of what he or she is feeling. If your verbal or nonverbal responses are grossly incongruent with the student's feelings, your ability to help may be nullified regardless of the quality of your advice. Along with making the student feel worse, he or she will simply tune you out.

As you provide acknowledgment by questioning and asking about different issues going on in students' lives, you are helping them think about more than just the encapsulated areas that have been bothering them. Also, by confirming your respect and understanding for students, you help them look at themselves differently and recognize that they do have some positive things going on in their lives.

Action

As the student discloses and you provide acknowledgment, you are also trying to determine what the student wants and needs from you and what you or others can provide. The student may need support, perspective, direction, or all three. Support means that the student may need to express some feelings, feel understood and listened to, and have his or her value as a human being confirmed by you. Perspective means that the student may need help seeing the problem in context, like recognizing the value of an alternative interpretation of the situation or seeing the "big picture" rather than simply focusing on the current, upsetting event. Too many self-doubts and too much emotion can impair problem-solving ability. By providing support and perspective, you can often help reduce the negative emotions enough so that the student can deal with the problem in a clear-headed, constructive way. Often, as you provide acknowledgment, you concurrently provide much support and perspective without even being aware of doing so.

Providing direction means leading the student to "try X." The X can be dropping a course, hiring a tutor, getting more information, going to the counseling center, or any of a multitude of solutions or steps toward a solution. There are several ways of providing direction. You might help the student reformulate a problem in order to come up with his or her own solution. You might provide new information or new interpretations that the student can take back and try out when the problem is next faced. Or you might refer the student to someone who can help better than you can. Whatever direction you arrive at, it is crucial that the student "own" it, even though you helped him or her get there. The student needs to be an integral part of choosing the direction rather than being told what to do. The more adequately the student has disclosed and you have acknowledged, the more readily the student will experience this sense of "ownership."

If lending your perspective does not seem to help, if you do not have any clear advice to give, and if you do not feel qualified or have the time or interest to help, referral is the next option to consider

Referral: General Information

Referral may be made to mental health professionals, deans, housing personnel, academic advisers, and the like. When you are faced with a student whom you feel you cannot help, for whatever reason, it is helpful to know about your campus's resources so that you can make appropriate referrals. Students often become discouraged and frustrated when they are sent on wild goose chases from office to office. If you are unsure whether a particular office is the appropriate place to send a student, call that office first to check; if possible, find out the name of a person to whom you may refer the student. Doing so not only communicates your personal concern to the student but models problem-solving skills and the legitimacy of not knowing all the answers.

When you are referring students for professional counseling, you should be prepared for resistance. Students sometimes feel that they should be able to work things out on their own, and they may react as though you are implying that they are "crazy" or "sick" if you suggest counseling. Your approach to the student and your personal attitude about counseling are extremely important at this point. It will help if you are familiar with the mental health services on your campus and can describe them matter-of-factly and with confidence.

Most college mental health services are specifically oriented to common problems students experience, and most of the students using the services have "normal" developmental problems related to learning to handle the unique pressures of the college environment. Leaving home, developing independence, changing relationships with family, forming personal value systems, managing emotions, developing a sense of competence, making new friends, choosing majors and careers, and dealing with academic work are only a few of the normal crises students face.

Along with remediation, most college mental health services emphasize prevention and development, such as working with students before their concerns develop into serious problems. With such broad-based emphases, it is easy to see that almost any student could benefit from an opportunity to discuss concerns with an interested, objective, nonjudgmental mental health professional. Through counseling, students will often gain fresh perspectives and uncover alternative, more productive ways of dealing with situations. Often one or two sessions suffice to help students feel more confident in tackling their problems.

This kind of general information about counseling can be reassuring to students who, in the absence of any experience with counseling, often hold negative stereotypes. If you or someone you know personally have been in counseling and found it helpful, sharing that information with a student reduces the stigma even further. If a respected and trusted person like you has seen a counselor, it must be okay!

Several other facts about your campus's mental health services will be helpful for you to know and convey to students during referral:

1. whether the service is free or if there is a charge for the service;
2. whether there are restrictions on the use of the service (e.g., must be currently enrolled, full vs. part-time student);
3. hours the service is available;
4. how to make an initial appointment (Does the service have walk-in hours? Are appointments made in advance? Can you send a student over to be seen right away? If so, under what conditions and how do you facilitate this?);
5. who the staff are (e.g., psychologists, social workers, advanced graduate students);
6. that all discussions are confidential except when the student is a danger to self or others; and
7. that no information about counseling can be released without the student's consent (usually in writing); therefore, no record of counseling will appear in the student's permanent files with the college or university.

With regard to these last two items you should check with your campus's mental health services for the specifics of their confidentiality policies.

How to make a referral. A student comes into your office, upset at having failed two of his first three chemistry exams. He begins to tell you (discloses) that he is in premed, that his father and mother are both physicians, and that he absolutely has to succeed in the chemistry class to have any chance of getting into medical school. Then he tells you that he is blanking out on the tests and having difficulty studying because he is so anxious.

As you talk to the student (acknowledgment), you and he clarify that (a) anxiety is interfering with both studying and test-taking skills, (b) it is extremely important to him to please his parents by following in their footsteps, and (c) he has given no thought to alternative career plans should he not be successful in premed. You are aware that there is a lot going on that defies a simple response, and you think that referral to a mental health professional would be a reasonable next step (action and referral). You might paraphrase in general terms what you have heard, summarizing the issues you think are contributing to the problem, and then say something like, "I think there is quite a lot going on here. You're not dealing with just the anxieties anyone feels going into a test but also with anxieties about pleasing your parents, anxieties about your future, and test anxiety. That's a lot of anxiety. I think you could use some help in sorting it out. I don't feel I have enough training to be helpful to you in dealing with this. But I am concerned about you, and what I'd really like is for you to talk to Mr./Ms./Dr._____ at the counseling center who is really helpful with these kinds of problems. Are you familiar with the counseling center's mental health services?" If the student is familiar with the services, you can ask for the student's reactions to your suggested referral and discuss any concerns with him. If the student is not familiar with the services you can tell him what you know about them and ask, "What do you think about talking with Mr./Ms./Dr._____?"

Your basic goal at this point is to communicate to the student your genuine concern and the reasons why you feel counseling might be beneficial. This approach is just as applicable for a student who does not disclose to you, but whose behavior concerns you, as it is for a student who comes to you with a problem.

Throughout your conversations with students, keep some general guidelines in mind:

1. *Be specific but nonjudgmental.* Tell the student exactly what behaviors have triggered your concern. "You're drinking too much" is a value judgment that a student readily dismisses whereas "You've come late to class every day this week, you've fallen asleep in class several

times, your test scores have dropped dramatically, and I'm concerned about you" is more to the point and harder to deny.

2. *Respond to the student as an interested, concerned friend rather than as an authority figure who knows what is right for the student.* Support the student for confiding in you. Use "I" statements like "I'm worried about you." Avoid "you" statements like "You should see a counselor" and instead say something like "I think counseling might be very helpful for you." Realizing that someone they respect is concerned and worried about them is often enough to shift the balance in favor of students' accepting a referral.

3. *Expect resistance or denial that the problem is "that serious."* If the person is reluctant to consider counseling or is uncomfortable with the idea, try to explore his or her concerns. Depending on the concerns, you may be able to provide reassurance or perspective by giving information about your campus's mental health services. If the person has had a bad previous experience with counseling or knows someone who has, be understanding that such experiences could make him or her skeptical or fearful. However, emphasize that you feel counseling is still an option that might work for him or her and that you will help to find someone with whom the student feels comfortable.

4. *Be matter-of-fact, respectful, and direct.* Do not try to minimize why you think help is needed. Never try to trick or deceive the student. Be clear that your referral represents your best judgment based on the information the student has given you or on the behaviors you have observed. Let the student know that you understand the problem, but respond honestly about whether you feel you can be of assistance.

5. *Know your campus's mental health resources.* As mentioned earlier, the more information you have about the mental health services on your campus the more you will be able to convey your confidence in the services and demystify the process for the student. It will be particularly helpful if you know the names of several counselors you can recommend. This conveys to the student that you are not abandoning him or her but rather are making a referral to someone you respect and trust. The likelihood that the student will follow through on your referral is therefore increased. If you must refer to an agency (e.g., the "Counseling Center") try to personalize it for the student as much as possible. One way to do that is to call the center's director, describe the student's situation, and elicit a recommendation with the student sitting in front of you. Along with in-

creasing the student's commitment, you convey the valid message that he or she is being considered individually.

6. *Leave the final decision to the student.* With the exception of emergencies, the student has the right to accept or refuse a referral to counseling. If the student emphatically says no or is extremely reluctant, express your understanding of those feelings and leave the door open for him or her to reconsider later. If the student seems on the fence, suggest that there is nothing to lose by going once; the student can always choose not to go back. But make it clear that it is the student's decision.

If the student seems amenable to a referral, you will have several choices to make about the best way to effect that referral. You might simply tell the student about the mental health services, provide some counselors' names if you have them, and suggest that the student make an appointment. With this approach you need to know the specific procedures preferred by the mental health services on your campus. Having the student make the initial contact gives him or her the responsibility for solving the problem and often increases commitment to counseling. At times, however, it may be preferable for you to call and make an appointment for the student. If you feel that the student is in crisis, is having difficulty thinking clearly, or will be unable to make contact personally, you may offer to do so. You might say, "I'd be glad to call the mental health service and set up an appointment for you. Would you like me to do that?" If the student agrees, call the service while the student is with you, tell the counselor or receptionist that you want to refer a student for problems with _____, and arrange the appointment. Tell the student the counselor's name, when and where to go, and let the student know that you will be interested in hearing how it goes. Support the student for making the decision to seek further help.

If a student is in crisis, you may want to go with that student to the mental health service to make sure he or she gets there. Under such circumstances, when possible, it is helpful to call first, tell who you are and that you have a student who you think needs to be seen immediately, and that you would like to bring that student over. Then you can work out procedures for doing so.

If you know that a student you're concerned about has accepted a referral and will be seeing a counselor, it is helpful if you call the counselor in advance of the appointment to provide whatever background information you have about the student's problems. It is not uncommon for students who were referred for suicidal feelings to come in and talk about something vague like minor study skills problems. Counselors are not mind readers!

The background you have can be helpful in orienting counselors to what to look for. Students may disclose more to you initially than to a counselor because (a) they know you, and (b) there is not the stigma associated with talking to you that there is to talking with a counselor. Use your judgment as to whether to make that call while the student is with you.

SOME HELPFUL HINTS TO REMEMBER

1. You need to hear and understand the problem before you can decide how to respond and whether to give support, facilitate perspective, or arrive at a direction. Do not skimp on disclosure and acknowledgment. If you jump in too quickly you are liable to shut students off.
2. You need to focus on the students' goals and values, not your own. For example, you might think a college education is essential, but for some students quitting school may be a responsible decision.
3. If your advice is not solicited in an obvious way, err toward providing support and perspective rather than direction. If students are looking for perspective, the questioning and understanding you do as you acknowledge should help them think about the larger context for the problems that have been bothering them. In providing perspective you need to be careful not to go overboard and encourage them to ignore their problems. Thus you need a fair amount of information about the rest of their lives to arrive at appropriate perspectives.
4. If students do seem to be seeking advice or direction, they are much more likely to try what you suggest if they feel you have listened to their problems adequately and taken them seriously. Otherwise they are liable to think you are just trying to brush them off.
5. Whether with disclosure, acknowledgment, support, perspective, or direction, there is a danger of fostering unhelpful dependency if you linger too long. You want students eventually to be able to function without you, so you want to send them off with the belief that they can do something for themselves.
6. Whether or not students accept your referrals, it is appropriate to show your continued interest in them at a later time by asking how things are going.

CONFIDENTIALITY AND YOU

The same confidentiality policy/law that protects the privacy of the students you refer for counseling will also prevent counselors from being able to tell you whether someone you referred for counseling is receiving help. In most states, if you call the mental health service to ask if a student is being seen for counseling, it is illegal for a staff member to give you any information without the student's written consent. This can be extremely frustrating when you are concerned about a student's well-being. Yet if counselors do not maintain this confidentiality, they will be ethically irresponsible and often legally liable. (In the unlikely instance where there is clear and present danger to someone's life, confidentiality can usually be broken.)

Awareness of this dilemma can lead to strategies that allow you to obtain feedback about a student you have referred. First, you can ask for follow-up information from the student. You can do this directly, by asking whether the student went to the mental health service, or indirectly, by asking the student to let you know if he or she decides to go. Second, when making an appointment for a student or when you take the student to the mental health service, you can mention to the counselor you wish follow-up information. Then the counselor can ask the student's permission to share follow-up information with you. Often this information will be limited to information about whether the student is being seen for counseling or information relevant to decisions you need to make about the student. When a student knows you are genuinely concerned, he or she will almost always agree to have the counselor release general information to you, while continuing to keep personal details private.

Remember, students you refer may not think to let you know whether they pursued counseling or whether it was helpful. You will probably need to take the initiative to let these students know you are interested in that information. You will also need to respect their rights to privacy should they not want any information about counseling released to you.

WHEN YOU'RE UNSURE ABOUT WHAT TO DO

At times you may be unsure whether students' problems are serious enough to warrant your concern. At other times students about whom you are very concerned may refuse to consider counseling. What do you do then? Contact the mental health services on your campus for consultation. The professional staff will frequently be able to help you evaluate the seriousness of a situation and recommend how you might proceed. Some brief collaborative problem solving can often ease your mind and result in better interactions with students. It is better to call and obtain assurance that a perceived problem is not serious than not to call at all.

ESSAYS ON COUNSELING ISSUES

Each of the essays in this section addresses a specific counseling issue: stress management, time management, procrastination, test anxiety, assertiveness, depression, and suicide prevention. This information can be used in many ways. Student affairs professionals familiar with counseling issues may use these essays as handouts to students and as "texts" for training student affairs colleagues, faculty, student paraprofessionals, and resident advisers. For readers unfamiliar with counseling issues, these essays provide self-help strategies that can be shared with students who have problems in these areas. These strategies often serve as a useful first step for students in confronting the problems addressed, and, when the strategies are not sufficient, as an indication that referral to a counselor may be helpful.

Four exams next week . . . stress. Three job interviews and they all want to know your life goals . . . stress. Troubles on the home front . . . stress. Your significant other wants to see someone else . . . stress.

"Stressed out!" You hear it every day and probably feel it nearly as often. Sometimes instant relief is available . . . you "blow it off" and let the four winds take their course. But more often than not, when you're stressed, it pervades your every bone—and it may hit your stomach and temples, too. When Tums and aspirin don't do the trick, some alternate strategies may be worth considering.

Stress isn't an all-or-none phenomenon, and neither are your responses to it. As your environment constantly changes, you continually adjust to these changes. With the death of someone close, election to student government, or an exciting new relationship, you experience stress as you readjust your life. Stress is the "wear and tear" on your body and soul that results from these adjustments. Stress has both positive and negative effects. Your body has evolved to "rise to the occasion," be the occasion climbing a tree to avoid being devoured by a lion, playing a tennis match, or saying "I do." As a positive influence, stress can compel you to action. "Getting psyched" is creating self-induced stress. But the negative effects are the ones you usually associate with stress. Stress can result in feelings of distrust, anger, rejection, and depression as well as health problems such as headaches, upset stomach, rashes, insomnia, ulcers, high blood pressure, heart disease, and strokes.

You can't avoid stress—but you can learn to manage it and use it to your advantage.

Maintaining yourself at *your* "optimal stress level" is a basic survival strategy. Sure, you'll go above and below this optimum when circumstances push you in either direction. But your goal is to find a middle ground that motivates but doesn't overwhelm. Remember, stress is not a bad thing. Positive stress leads to excitement and anticipation. Meeting challenges and even dealing with frustration and disappointments can add depth and enrichment to your life. At the other end of the spectrum, too little stress for too long acts as a depressant and may lead to boredom and apathy. Too much stress, though, will leave anyone "tied up in knots."

But what's too much or too little? Not all people are alike. If you thrive on action, a routine and stable job could be stressful, not to mention boring and depressing. On the other hand, if stability puts you into your comfort zone, a job that requires lots of new and diverse duties may stress you to the max. Finding your own optimal stress level is the trick here.

When you experience the symptoms of stress, you're beyond your optimum. Unrelieved stress, outside the boundaries of your optimum, is often related to physical illness. If this becomes the case, you need to reduce the stress in your life or improve your ability to manage it. You can change the source of the stress or change your reactions. Either case requires a total effort toward change. How do you do it? Here are some tips:

- Become aware of the things that stress you and your reactions, both physical and emotional, to these stressors. Don't ignore them. It won't work. Your body will still react. Your best bet is to figure out what events bother you and then figure out why. Pay attention to your body's responses. Do you get physically upset or nervous? In what specific ways?
- Some things can be changed—some can't. Figure out which ones are under your control. Can you avoid your stressors or eliminate them? Can you reduce their intensity? Can you reduce their duration by taking a vacation or study break? Are you willing to take the time to change things by learning to manage your time better, setting achievable goals, and getting interpersonal matters on course?
- Try to reduce your emotional reactions to stress. Do you exaggerate the possible effects of your stressors? Do you magnify a difficult situation into a disaster? Do you expect to please everyone and get hit from all sides at once in a no-win situation? Do you overreact, viewing everything as critical and urgent? Give yourself a break—put things into perspective. Try to see the stressor as something you can cope with, not as a force that overpowers your life.
- Don't abuse your body. Run-down physical reserves heighten your adverse reactions to stress. Exercising, eating right, avoiding stimulants like nicotine and excessive caffeine, mixing leisure with work, and getting enough sleep on a consistent schedule are within most folks' control.
- Use basic techniques to get your physical reactions under control. Pounding heart and increased breathing rate? Try slow, deep breathing. Learn some relaxation techniques—stretching, yoga, meditation, biofeedback. Your doctor's prescription drugs may help for the short term, but they're not a good long-term answer. Learning to do it yourself is a better road.
- Maintain your emotional reserves. Be your own best friend—listen to yourself and your feelings when you make decisions about your own life. Expect to be down or frustrated now and then—sometimes it's natural. Develop some mutually supportive friendships.
- Make sure your goals are your own. Imposed goals can drive you bananas.

Above all, remember, with a few preventive strategies you can prevent stress from becoming distress.

There's always been this person next door, or two rows over, or at the next lab bench who seems to be able to get 1,001 things done each semester when you have a hard time even getting out of bed, much less getting your daily assignments done. Highly motivated people? Maybe. But if you ask them you'll probably find that they're just good time managers—even though they may not realize it. What's their secret? Motivation surely plays a role, but there are other important things.

Successful time management is the secret to accomplishing the things that must get done, and better yet, the things that you want to get done. The secret can be unlocked and put to use with the right attitude and techniques.

The issue of who controls your life is one key to examine. Many aspects of your life are under your control, but only you can activate the control button. If you think your life is completely controlled by external events, you have given up self-control. You're probably always looking for external signals to motivate you, like deadlines and others' expectations. This is a passive approach. Sure, you must respond to many externals, but how you do this should be under your own control. For example, how you meet those deadlines and how much you participate is up to you. You can anticipate how you want to get different things done and when. Then you can create your own timetable. That's control.

You need to develop a healthy attitude about your ability to control your own time. You *can* miss that next television special, that new movie, the band that your friends are going to see at your favorite bar, or that next organization meeting. You'll find that your friends still like you and that you're still up-to-date on what's going on. You don't have to shape yourself to others' expectations. In fact, you can't meet everyone's expectations, nor should you. They may be poorly timed, inappropriate for you, of a different priority, or even impossible. You have to consider your own needs first and measure them on your own yardstick. Then you can create your own timeframe.

You also have to know your limits. Perfectionists, for instance, find it difficult to complete tasks because perfection is impossible to achieve. Having reasonable expectations allows you the freedom to set time management goals that are within your grasp. Otherwise you set yourself up for failure.

Beyond attitude, you need to be aware of your own biological rhythms and integrate them into your patterns. Don't plan to get up at 5 a.m. to cram if you're useless until noon. Take advantage of times when your energy levels are highest, and do your most demanding work then. Be aware of your work environment; keep it conducive to concentration. For some, a nearby bed and stereo are deadly. And beware of rewarding yourself for intention rather than progress. Don't say, "Because I've decided to write a paper tomorrow I deserve to go to a party tonight." Rewarding intention can destroy your motivation to begin. Instead, reward yourself for progress, including completion of components of larger tasks.

109

But what about specific strategies? You'll eventually want to develop your own style of managing things, but consider these techniques:

- What's your overview? For example, what do you want to accomplish during a given semester? Start by considering everything—school as well as personal and social activities. Then consider what your important goals are. What's of immediate concern and what can be postponed? Be realistic.
- Construct a timetable by anticipating deadlines and foreseeable crises. Plan for them. Plan on delays and allow time for them in your calendar. If you don't use a calendar, try one. Then work backward and consider each week as a subcategory to be planned.
- Add lower priority items into your schedule after you've planned for what you really need to get done.
- Identify specific goals for each week and rate their relative importance: What has to get done (A), what it would be nice to get done (B), and the also-rans (C). Then reclassify the Bs into As or Cs so that you're not distracted by nonessentials.
- Don't get bogged down with C tasks. When they interfere, skip them or delegate them. If you type with one finger get somebody to type your papers, and send your laundry home to Uncle Max.
- Finally, review your A activities and determine the steps you need to follow to accomplish each one. Break down larger activities into a series of self-starter units. Be realistic! Consider whether you have the luxury to do everything the ideal way. Trim the fat and get going.

This method is based on the "80/20 rule," which states that 80% of the value of doing a typical list of activities comes from doing the most important 20%. By setting priorities this way, if you get 20% of your tasks done you've achieved 80% of your goals. Not bad, huh?

You'll also have to deal with your environment. Shove those time wasters and interruptions into a locked closet. Safeguard and covet those essential blocks of work time. Even 10 minutes can be useful if you've planned your tasks well. Learn to say "No." Interruptions not only interfere, but they also put you on edge to expect further interruptions. Clear your visual field; keep your back to the "traffic flow"; keep your door closed. Find a place to hide away—obscure libraries or classrooms where your friends can't find you. Unplug your phone or tell people you'll call them back. Above all, be practical! Keep in mind such mundane things as library hours, bus schedules, and turnaround time for the computer.

Remember to be wary of waiting for clear-cut signals like deadlines and others' expectations to motivate you—you're likely to end up feeling confused, compromised, frustrated, and wondering what's wrong with you that you don't ever follow through. You *can* have control over many aspects of your life, but you and you alone are responsible for exercising that control. But be careful not to let organizing become your overriding goal. Beyond a certain point, adding techniques may simply become another way of procrastinating. Keep things in a healthy perspective. Now get out there and take control!

Exam tomorrow—"Oh, it can wait a few more hours; I think I'll watch the tube for a while." Paper due on Friday—"Not to worry—I think I'll take in a movie tonight."

Procrastination . . . all-nighters, rush jobs, emotions of guilt and anxiety, and feelings of stupidity, inadequacy, and laziness. Not to mention the value judgments: "I'm a procrastinator, there's something wrong with me. I'm worthless." Makes it sound like you're doomed for life. That's a pretty stiff penalty for going to a movie.

Procrastination comes in different shapes and sizes. It may come from a lack of time management or study skills. It may be a problem of understanding what's expected of you in courses. Maybe it's a fear of venturing into new realms or feeling unable to handle a task. Maybe you see no personal relevance in anything you're doing: Your coursework seems meaningless or you never wanted to bother with college. Or possibly the major you're in is not what you want to do, but you feel pressured into it by family or peers or a mistaken belief that if you don't follow a certain track you'll be left high and dry in the job market. Maybe you're a perfectionist and your standards are impossible.

Whatever your story, it comes down to an emotional problem of why you procrastinate and a mechanical problem of how—what form your procrastination takes. Consider these scenarios: Do any of them sound like you?

- You ignore the task as if it'll go away . . . No matter how many pennies you throw in the well, that chem midterm just won't vaporize.
- You tell yourself you grasp concepts so quickly that you'll only need an hour for 6 hours' worth of computer science problem sets . . . The amount of time it takes to get the job done won't change. Be careful not to underestimate the work involved or overestimate your abilities.
- Do you substitute one activity for another? . . . Not all things are equal—a clean apartment may be nice but not when cleaning time competes with paper writing time.
- Minor delays accumulate . . . Putting off studying to watch prime time TV could get you into late night talk shows before you wake up on the couch wondering what happened to last night.
- Do you fill your pack with books, trudge to the library through a tornado, and brag about the fact that there's so much you're going to do until all of a sudden the library attendant tells you it's closing time? . . . Dramatizing your commitment to work is often a way of avoiding doing it.
- Do you convince yourself that mediocre performance and lowered standards are acceptable? . . . A 2.95 GPA won't get you into the med school of your choice. And pretending it doesn't matter can keep you from making the decision to work harder.
- Do you write and rewrite the first paragraph ad nauseum . . . and never get around to the second?

- Do alternative choices paralyze you . . . can't decide which topic to choose so you don't choose at all?

Here you are folks. Stuck. What comes next?

1. Admit you have a problem.
2. Identify the form(s) your procrastination takes and write them down.
3. Analyze the causes. Be honest with yourself. If you want to spend only a minimal amount of effort or time on a particular task, admit it. And don't let guilt feelings get in the way of this realization. Weigh the consequences of various amounts of effort in terms of the outcomes you want and find the optimal return for your investment.
4. If you've been avoiding work unintentionally, this is turnaround time. Admit to yourself that you do want to seek certain goals, accept the responsibilities, and go for it.
5. Figure out the time-based reality. How long does it really take to get a certain task completed? How much time do you have to spend? Figure out how much energy you use to get psyched to get going and how much energy you actually need to do the task. Achieve a healthy balance. Don't get stuck dramatizing your commitment at the expense of getting down to business.
6. Put together a strategy. Create an overview of the entire project and the steps necessary go get it done.

Strategy planning is essential, especially for larger and more involved projects.

- Break the task into smaller parts; you're less likely to get overwhelmed if you attack your work one step at a time.
- Take these small steps and put them into a reasonable timeframe. Be careful not to fool yourself here about how much time you'll need.
- Reward yourself for *completing* these small steps—not for starting them. Allowing yourself some variety and relaxation after you've accomplished something will make you less resentful of the work that still needs to be done.
- Monitor your progress on these small steps. Watch for the pitfalls we talked about and catch yourself immediately so you don't get stuck again. Keep track of the whole picture.
- Be reasonable in your self-expectations. Perfectionistic or overwhelmingly great expectations may cause you to rebel and bushwhack the whole tomato.

Now get going. Don't label yourself a procrastinator as though it's a personality characteristic you got through your gene pool. You procrastinate. It's a problem. But you *can* do something about it.

What's one more lousy test? "It's everything . . . it's my whole future . . . it's a definitive measure of my self-worth and intellectual capacity . . . if I flunk I'm a Class-A dummy!" If this sounds familiar when hourlies and finals come up—welcome to test anxiety.

Pounding heart . . . cold clammy hands . . . upset stomach . . . extreme muscle tension . . . lump in the throat. All these can be symptoms of test anxiety. And although some degree of this nervous energy is needed to motivate you for tests, when it becomes so overwhelming that panic sets in, you've entered a new ball game. When it comes to tests, panic may not show itself in pulling your hair out. It may show itself in other ways—sleeping through an exam, going blank in front of the test paper even though you know the material cold, or simply "the old choke."

You don't want to be so mellowed out that you're nonchalant going into an exam. Some nervous energy is needed to keep you in high gear and ready to do your best. But if keeping that energy level at an optimal level is a problem, here are some thoughts.

Test anxiety takes two basic forms: If you're unprepared for the test, your anxiety is a normal, rational reaction; if you're prepared but still overreact or panic, your reaction is *not* rational. It's helpful to know which type of anxiety you have because overcoming the effects may involve different strategies.

Good preparation is a key factor. We all know that. You may want to begin by talking to your professors about what they look for on the tests they write. This is not the same thing as finding out what questions are going to be asked. Many times students screw up exams and begin to freak out because they don't understand what a professor is looking for; they don't understand what's behind the test itself. One sure way to deal with this is to talk to them. They aren't out to get you, and they may have better insight into your problem with their tests than you think. Often they'll know you are a better student than your tests indicate, and you can usually depend on them to work with you to figure out where your misunderstanding with your exam rests.

One key to beating test anxiety is to focus that nervous energy on preparing for the test. Consider these tips to help you prepare:

- Avoid cramming. The day before a test is not the time to master large amounts of material, and trying to do so can produce a lot of anxiety. Instead, pace yourself and organize your time. Build a schedule that's realistic and flexible. Allow enough time to pull the pieces together into a coherent whole.
- Try to master the main concepts of the course by combining the information you've been presented throughout the semester.
- As you study, consider what some likely test questions might be and practice answering them by integrating material from lectures, notes, and texts.
- Take care of your body. Focus on the basic needs of sleep, exercise, diet,

and a spice of recreation. Now is not the time to let your body do a fast boogie to Destructoville. Your mind needs your body for basic survival.

- Reward yourself as you study; take measured breaks that have predetermined beginnings and endings.
- If you're short on time, set priorities: Study the basic stuff first and save the filler for later; get the general picture and then fill in the details.
- Decide on a reward for yourself for after the test and follow through with it no matter how you feel you've done.
- If you can't cover all of the material, select a part that you can cover well and set a goal of presenting what you do know on the test.

Now let's consider attitude. Your overall attitude toward tests certainly can affect how you react to them. Tests per se don't cause anxiety, your perceptions of tests do. The importance of any one test rests primarily in your mind. You can't change the test, but you can change the way you think about it. How you perform on any one test won't determine whether your parents make you sleep in the garage, whether you're a good person, or whether you get into graduate school. If you put each test into a slightly less catastrophic framework, you'll do wonders at keeping your anxiety under control.

Your most reasonable expectation when you actually take the test is to show as much as you can about what you know. Avoid thinking of yourself in a negative sense. Remind yourself that a test is only a test—not a measure of your worth as a human being.

Remember, too, that tests vary in what they actually measure. Some are good, but some are really goofy. They may not measure your ability to think creatively or even your understanding of the material. Sometimes the nature of the test has more to do with who wrote it than with the material you're being tested on. And sometimes your ability to do well on a test has more to do with how you relate to the way the test is written than to how well you've studied. What that test does measure is how well you can take that test.

The day of the test:

- Make sure you've gotten plenty of sleep the night before the test. Being rested enables you to think sharply, synthesize, and recall.
- Don't cram up to the last minute; it creates confusion.
- Don't eat erratically—there's nothing like a rumbling belly to distract you or a full one to put you to sleep. Don't overdose on coffee or sugar.
- Relax the hour before the test: Try a hot shower, a long walk, or your favorite tunes.
- Know where the test room is. Arrive 10 minutes early, get a good seat, and settle in with a magazine. Stay away from those crazy foot tappers and teeth grinders or any other distractions.
- Dress comfortably; baggies are great for sitting and several layers will prepare you for the variable heat conditions.

Once you get the test in hand:

- Review the whole thing first. Read the directions twice. Don't be afraid to ask questions if you don't understand. Read each question, and make sure you understand what each question asks. Again, don't be afraid to ask your prof to explain a question to you. Map out a time schedule for answering the parts—work on the easiest parts first to get the ball rolling.
- Make an outline for essay questions and exams. Rambling wastes time and graders look for answers that are to the point, regardless of length. Unsure of the correct response on a multiple choice question? Mark the margin and come back to it later. Beware of tricky qualifying words, such as "only," "always," or "most."
- Don't rush. Use a watch to pace yourself, but don't let your watch pressure you. If you don't have enough time, make a strategy to maximize your score. Maybe you'll want to do well on parts you know, maybe you'll go for the high point questions.

If anxiety continues:

- Get a drink or go to the bathroom.
- Remember the postexam reward you've promised yourself.
- Tell yourself "I can be anxious later, after I've taken the test."
- Take a few slow deep breaths to relax and stay positive.

If you try all these tips and still have too much anxiety, you may need additional help. Contact your campus's counseling service and ask for someone who can help with test anxiety. They're used to it, trained to help, and can probably get you back on track quite quickly.

At times you may have found that communicating your needs is not an easy task. Yet the ability to get the things you need—information, services, advice, favors, or whatever—is a powerful skill to help you reach your goals.

You've no doubt run into people who speak out and say what they want. Sometimes you admire them for that ability, and sometimes they really make you mad. Sometimes what they say seems like a reasonable request, but the way it's said makes your hackles rise in anger. There's a fine line that divides assertiveness and aggressiveness, but reactions to the two are clearly distinguishable. "Hey roomie, go down to the vending machine and get me a Coke" is sure to get a different reaction than "I'm bushed, would you get me a Snickers at the snack bar?"

Most of the time no one's going to read your mind. You'll have to say what you want. On the other hand, you may be afraid that if you do, you'll turn people off. That's the fine line again. Being assertive is the ability to express yourself and your rights without violating the rights of others. It "basically means the ability to express your thoughts and feelings in a way that clearly states your needs and keeps the lines of communication open" (Ryan & Travis, 1981, p. 174).

When you act assertively you will feel more self-confident. Generally, you will also gain the respect of your peers and friends, and the impression you make on professors and job supervisors will improve, too. At the interpersonal level, assertiveness is a great skill. Chances for honest relationships are greater because you are communicating what you truly need and feel. You'll probably feel much better about yourself and about your self-control in everyday situations. This, in turn, will improve your decision-making ability and, probably, your chances for getting what you really want from life.

It's not always easy to express your needs. Before you can do so comfortably, you have to believe you have a legitimate right to those needs. You do have certain rights. Keep them in mind.

You have the right:

- to decide how to lead your life; this includes pursuing your own goals and dreams and establishing your own priorities;
- to have your own values, beliefs, opinions, and emotions—and the right to respect yourself for them, no matter the opinion of others;
- not to justify or explain your actions or feelings to others;
- to tell others how you wish to be treated;
- to express yourself and to say, "No," "I don't know," "I don't understand," or even "I don't care." You have the right to take the time you need to formulate your ideas before expressing them;
- to ask for information or help without having negative feelings about your needs;
- to change your mind, to make mistakes, and sometimes to act illogically, with full understanding and acceptance of the consequences;

- to like yourself even though you're not perfect, and sometimes to do less than you are capable of doing;
- to have positive, satisfying relationships within which you feel comfortable and free to express yourself honestly, and the right to change or end relationships if they don't meet your needs; and
- to change, enhance, or develop your life in any way you may determine.

You probably won't be assertive if you don't believe you have these rights. Instead, you may react passively to circumstances and events in your life. You can wind up feeling hurt, anxious, and angry when you let the needs, opinions, and judgments of others become more important than your own. The kinds of passive or nonassertive behaviors you have going on here are frequently indirect, emotionally dishonest, and self-denying—probably the opposite of what you really intended.

But maybe you figure that it's better than being selfish. Lots of people fear that when they attend to their legitimate needs and when they assert their rights they're being concerned only about their own rights, with little or no regard for those of others. In other words, they're being selfish. Not true. Your rights and other people's rights are interrelated; concern for your rights implicitly involves concern for the rights of others, too.

In fact, when you behave selfishly or in a way that violates the rights of others, you're acting in a destructive, aggressive manner. It's that fine line again. Destructive/aggressive versus constructive/assertive. Remember, assertiveness is a constructive process. Aggressiveness means expressing your own rights, but at the expense, degradation, or humiliation of another. Emotional or physical force is used so powerfully that the rights of others are not allowed to surface. You may get what you want, in the short run, but aggressiveness usually causes strong reactions like anger and vengeance. It works against your long-range intentions and causes people to lose respect for you. Aggressiveness is a power trip; assertiveness is an attempt at communication and mutuality.

But keep your hat on—assertiveness won't solve all your problems. It won't guarantee you happiness or fair treatment by others; it won't solve all your personal problems and guarantee that others will be assertive rather than aggressive. But it will increase your chances of getting what you want and it may help reduce the conflicts you have in relationships.

Assertiveness is a strong tool for improving communication, a tool you have to learn to use. You don't just open your mouth and spout asssertive sentences at the first try. You need to know some techniques and practice them until they become new habits. Here are a few:

1. Be as specific and clear as possible about what you want, think, and feel. Project this preciseness as part of how you frame your statements:
   "I want to . . ."
   "I don't want you to . . ."
   "Would you . . . ?"
   "I liked it when you did that."

"I have a different opinion. I think that . . ."

"I have mixed reactions. I agree with this aspect for these reasons, but I am disturbed about that aspect for these reasons."

Sometimes it's helpful to explain exactly what you mean and what you don't mean, such as "I'm not interested in getting a resume item, Professor Jones. I want to work in your lab so I can learn some skills." Or, in another context, "I don't want to break up over this issue. I just want to talk it over to see if we can prevent it from happening again."

2. Be direct. Don't toss your statements to the world in hopes that they'll reach the intended person. Deliver the message in person. If you want to tell something to Chris, tell Chris; don't tell everyone except Chris and don't tell it to Chris's friends.

3. It's your message, so "own" it. When you make your statements, acknowledge that they are from *your* frame of reference, *your* concept of right versus wrong or good versus bad, *your* perceptions. One way to acknowledge ownership is with the personalized "I" statement. You can, for instance, say "I don't agree with you" as compared with "You're wrong," or "I'd like you to clean up the bathroom" as compared with "You really should clean up the bathroom." In one case, you're suggesting that someone is wrong or bad and should change for their own benefit. In the other case, you're suggesting that it will please you. The former case usually fosters resentment and resistance, the latter, understanding and cooperation.

4. Ask for feedback. Communication is a two-way process. "Am I being clear?" "What's your opinion?" "How do you see all this?" "What do you want to do?" Asking for feedback accomplishes several goals. It can encourage others to correct any misconceptions that you may have; it can help others realize you are expressing an opinion, feeling, or desire—not a demand; and it can encourage others to be clear, direct, and specific in their feedback to you.

Remember in all of your efforts to become assertive that it's a skill, and it must be practiced. It's not just the words you say, however; the nonverbals are important, too. How you communicate with voice tone, gestures, posture, eye contact, and facial expressions will all have an effect. Time, practice, and a willingness to accept yourself as you make mistakes are all part of the process. Once you learn to be assertive you will have invaluable skills to use in pursuing your life goals. You may not choose to be assertive in every situation, but the skills will be there if you need them. It's definitely worth the effort! Try it— the rewards will be there.

Most everyone feels "down" once in a while. It's a natural feeling that usually has a minimal effect on your normal everyday activities and goes away quickly. Most people can deal with this feeling when it isn't too intense. But feelings of depression can run through a continuum of intensity and severity. Depression can be deep and long lasting, sometimes for months or even years. It can affect your ability to deal with daily activities—you can still cope, but it's difficult. And it can become so intense that suicide may seem to be the only solution.

Depression is a disturbance in mood. It is characterized by varying degrees of sadness, disappointment, loneliness, hopelessness, self-doubt, and guilt.

When depression is extremely severe, your moods may undergo large-scale fluctuations; you may want to withdraw completely from daily routine or the outside world.

Depression can affect your life in many ways. What can you look out for?

1. changes in feeling or perceptions:
   • crying spells or, at the other extreme, lack of emotional responsiveness;
   • inability to find pleasure in anything;
   • feelings of hopelessness or worthlessness;
   • exaggerated sense of guilt or self-blame;
   • loss of sexual desire; and
   • loss of warm feelings toward family or friends.

2. changes in behavior and attitudes:
   • lack of interest in prior activities and withdrawal from other people;
   • neglect of responsibilities and appearance;
   • irritability, complaints about matters previously taken in stride;
   • dissatisfaction with life in general;
   • impaired memory, inability to concentrate, indecisiveness, and confusion; and
   • reduced ability to cope on a daily basis.

3. physical complaints:
   • chronic fatigue and lack of energy;
   • complete loss of appetite, or at the other extreme, compulsive eating;
   • insomnia, early morning wakefulness, or excessive sleeping;
   • unexplained headaches, backaches, and similar complaints; and
   • digestive problems including stomach pain, nausea, indigestion, or change in bowel habits.

Where does depression come from? Well, it doesn't just fly in from Los Angeles to spend the weekend. Frequently, you can identify the source. Maybe it's the loss of a loved one or a breakup of an important relationship. When the source is readily apparent and you're aware of it, the odds are that the depression will become less intense over time and eventually fade away. But when the source isn't apparent or is unclear, the depression can get worse because you're unable to understand it. The resulting sense of loss of control can then add to the actual feelings of depression.

Depression can be seen as a withdrawal from physical or psychological stress. Identifying and understanding the causes of this stress are necessary steps in learning to cope with depression.

So you're depressed—what can you do to help yourself?

- Be honest with yourself as you analyze your mood changes so you can identify your stressors. What's troubling you? Relationship problems? Try to work them out with the people involved or find an understanding friend to talk to.
- Change your normal routine even if you don't feel like it. Get into something new; do your favorite activities.
- Exercise to work off tension and help you relax. Maybe even tire yourself out so you can get some good sleep.
- Avoid your known stressors.
- Try not to make long-term commitments, decisions, or changes that make you feel trapped or confined; put them off until you feel you're ready to cope.
- Talk to a counselor or to a physician if physical complaints persist.

How about depressed friends—what can you do? You may be a life-saver. A severely depressed friend may become withdrawn, passive, self-absorbed, and even suicidal. Tell your friend of your concern for his or her well-being. Problems may come into the open. Your primary goal is to let your friend know that you're concerned and willing to help.

As you talk, keep these points in mind:

- Don't try to "cheer up" your friend—it discounts the reality of the depression.
- Don't criticize or shame your friend—blaming him or her for the depression doesn't help.
- Don't sympathize and claim that you feel the same way—you don't and your friend will see this dishonesty.
- Try not to get angry with a depressed person—it creates distance, not closeness.

There comes a time when friends aren't enough. They just don't have the skills. Don't try to be a professional shrink. If feelings of depression turn to thoughts of suicide, urge your friend to see a professional. If your friend resists, seek out professional help yourself so you will know how to deal with the situation.

Consult a mental health professional:

- when pain or problems outweigh pleasures much of the time;
- when symptoms are so severe and persistent that day-to-day functioning is impaired; or
- when stress is so overwhelming that suicide seems to be a viable option.

A mental health professional can help identify the causes and sources of depression and help the individual find ways to overcome them.

Suicide is the second leading cause of death among college students (after accidents). Chances are that you've thought about suicide at some time in your life or that you will encounter a friend or acquaintance with suicidal thoughts or feelings while you're in college. Understanding some facts about suicide will leave you better prepared should you encounter someone with suicidal feelings or impulses.

The common link among people who kill themselves is the belief that suicide is the *only* solution to a set of overwhelming feelings. The attraction of suicide is that it will finally end these unbearable feelings. The tragedy of suicide is that intense emotional distress often blinds people to alternative solutions—yet other solutions are almost always available.

We all experience feelings of loneliness, depression, helplessness, and hopelessness from time to time. The death of a family member, the breakup of a relationship, blows to our self-esteem, feelings of worthlessness, or major financial setbacks are serious problems that all of us may have to face at some point in our lives. Because each person's emotional makeup is unique, each of us responds to situations differently. In considering whether a person may be suicidal, it is imperative that the crisis be evaluated from that person's perspective. What may seem of minor importance to you can be of major importance to someone else—and an event that may be insignificant to you can be extremely distressful to another. Regardless of the nature of the crisis, if a person feels overwhelmed, there is danger that suicide may seem an attractive solution.

Danger signals. At least 70% of all people who commit suicide give some clue to their intentions before they make an attempt. Becoming aware of these clues and the severity of the person's problems can help prevent such a tragedy. If a person you know is going through a particularly stressful situation—perhaps having difficulty maintaining a meaningful relationship, consistently failing in meeting preset goals, or even experiencing stress at having failed an important test—watch for other signs of crisis.

Many persons convey their intentions directly with statements such as "I feel like killing myself," or "I don't know how much longer I can take this." Others in crisis may hint at a detailed suicide plan with statements such as "I've been saving up my pills in case things get really bad," or "Lately I've been driving my car like I really don't care what happens." In general, statements describing feelings of depression, helplessness, extreme loneliness, or hopelessness may suggest suicidal thoughts. It is important to listen to these "cries for help" because they are usually desperate attempts to communicate to others the need to be understood and helped.

Persons thinking about suicide often show outward changes in their behavior. They may prepare for death by giving away prized possessions, making a will, or putting other affairs in order. They may withdraw from those around them, change eating or sleeping patterns, or lose interest in prior activities or relationships. A sudden, intense lift in spirits may also be a danger signal, as it may indicate the person already feels a sense of relief knowing the problems will "soon be ended."

Myths about suicide. Myth: "You have to be crazy to even think about suicide."

Fact: Most people have thought of suicide from time to time. Most suicides and suicide attempts are made by intelligent, temporarily confused individuals who are expecting too much of themselves, especially in the midst of a crisis.

Myth: "Once a person has made a serious suicide attempt, that person is unlikely to make another."

Fact: The opposite is often true. Persons who have made prior suicide attempts may be at a greater risk of actually committing suicide; for some, suicide attempts may seem easier a second or third time.

Myth: "If a person is seriously considering suicide, there is nothing you can do."

Fact: Most suicidal crises are time-limited and based on unclear thinking. Persons attempting suicide want to escape from their problems. Instead of escaping, they need to confront their problems directly in order to find other solutions—solutions that can be found with the help of concerned individuals who support them through the crisis period until they are able to think more clearly.

Myth: "Talking about suicide may give a person the idea."

Fact: A crisis situation and the resulting emotional distress will already have triggered the thought in a vulnerable person. Your openness and concern in asking about suicide will allow the person experiencing pain to talk about the problem, which may help reduce his or her anxiety. This may also allow the person with suicidal thoughts to feel less lonely or isolated, and, perhaps, a bit relieved.

How You Can Help. Most suicides can be prevented by sensitive responses to the person in crisis. If you think someone you know may be suicidal, you should:

- Remain calm. In most instances, there is no rush. Sit and listen—really listen to what the person is saying. Give understanding and active emotional support for his or her feelings.
- Deal directly with the topic of suicide. Most individuals have mixed feelings about death and dying and are open to help. Don't be afraid to ask or talk directly about suicide.
- Encourage problem solving and positive actions. Remember that the person involved in emotional crisis is not thinking clearly. Encourage him or her to refrain from making any serious, irreversible decisions while in a crisis. Talk about the positive alternatives that may establish hope for the future.
- Get assistance. Although you want to help, do not take full responsibility by trying to be the sole counsel. Seek out resources that can lend qualified help, even if it means breaking a confidence. Let the troubled person know you are concerned—so concerned that you are willing to arrange help beyond what you can offer.

UCLA suicide prevention experts have summarized the information to be conveyed to a person in crisis as follows:

"The suicidal crisis is *temporary*. Unbearable pain can be *survived*. *Help* is available. You are *not alone*."

EPILOGUE

We started this book with a metaphor about road travel. We suggested that good education involves more than speeding along the superhighways of college. We argued in favor of back-roads travel because what is learned in the process of this kind of travel can be just as important as getting to a destination. The enriching features of back-roads travel come from taking time to look around and from stopping along the way to talk with the locals. Such conversations are likely to lead to altered routes in order to try out new leads and, perhaps, find something attractive along the way that might have been missed.

Deliberately missing from our original metaphor was a compass. This book is that compass. It is meant to serve as a pointer to some of the hidden resources and rationales of colleges and universities.

With this compass, advice givers can help students learn to map their own educations so that they can incorporate more than superhighway travel. If this advice-giving process is successful, students become their own map makers. And as they leave the guidance of their advice givers, they become self-guiding. That, after all, is what education is all about.

EPILOGUE

REFERENCES

Arons, A.B. (1985). "Critical thinking" and the baccalaureate curriculum. *Liberal Education, 71*, 141–157.

Association of American Medical Colleges. (1984). *Medical school admissions requirements* 1985–1986. Washington, DC: Author.

Bechtel, D.S. (1984). *Early career patterns of humanities college graduates: One institution's perspective of the "lean years," 1972–1981*. Urbana: University of Illinois Career Development and Placement Center.

Bronowski, J. (1965). *Science and human values*. New York: Harper & Row.

Cheney, L.V. (1986, September 1). Students of success. *Newsweek*, p. 7.

Ender, S.C., Winston, R.B., & Miller, T.K. (1984). Academic advising reconsidered. In R.B. Winston, T.K. Miller, S.C. Ender, T.J. Grites, & Associates, *Developmental academic advising* (pp. 3–34). San Francisco: Jossey-Bass.

Grites, T.J. (1979). *Academic advising: Getting us through the eighties*. Washington, DC: American Association for Higher Education—Educational Resources Information Center (AAHE-ERIC), Higher Education Research Report No. 7.

Heppner, M.J., & Johnson, J.A. (1985). Computerized guidance and information systems. *Journal of College Student Personnel, 26*, 156–163.

Jacobson, R.L. (1986, February 5). Most students are satisfied with their education, survey indicates, but frustrations are widespread. *Chronicle of Higher Education*, pp. 1, 27–31.

Katchadourian, H.A., & Boli, J. (1985). *Careerism and intellectualism among college students*. San Francisco: Jossey-Bass.

Lauer, R.M., & Hussey, M. (1986). A new way to become educated. *The Humanist, 46*(1), 5–7, 41.

Neusner, J. (1984). *How to grade your professors*. Boston: Beacon Press.

Perry, W., Jr. (1970). *Intellectual and ethical development in the college years*. New York: Holt, Rinehart and Winston.

Ryan, R.S., & Travis, J.W. (1981). *The wellness workbook*. Berkeley: Ten Speed Press.

Study finds small businesses ignore computer skills in hiring. (1986, April 30). *Chronicle of Higher Education*, p. 28.

Watkins, B.T. (1986, January 5). For Ph.D. holders in the humanities, success in business seen based on graduate skills, not knowledge. *Chronicle of Higher Education*, pp. 23–25.

Winston, R.B., Miller, T.K., Ender, S.C., Grites, T.J., & Associates. (1984). *Developmental academic advising*. San Francisco: Jossey-Bass.